The Birth of the English Common Law

The Birth of the
English
Common Law

R. C. VAN CAENEGEM

*Professor of Medieval History and of Legal History
in the University of Ghent*

CAMBRIDGE UNIVERSITY PRESS

Published by the Syndics of the Cambridge University Press
Bentley House, 200 Euston Road, London NW1 2DB
American Branch: 32 East 57th Street, New York, N.Y.10022

© Cambridge University Press 1973

Library of Congress Catalogue Card Number: 72–89812

ISBN: 0 521 20097 0

First published 1973
Reprinted 1974

First printed in Great Britain by
Western Printing Services Ltd, Bristol
Reprinted in Great Britain by
REDWOOD BURN LIMITED
Trowbridge & Esher

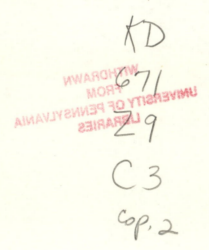

Contents

Conjugi carissimae
laboris semper sociae

Preface

While I was staying in Cambridge as a Visiting Fellow of University College, whose warm hospitality I would like to acknowledge, the Faculty of History invited me to give a series of four lectures. I accepted the invitation with pleasure and the Faculty agreed that I should talk of the formative years of the Common Law of England. I felt that the students might find it useful to hear, in the succinct and – I hope – accessible form of lectures, some views I had expounded in a more elaborate and detailed way in my *Royal Writs in England from the Conquest to Glanvill* (London, 1959). I also welcomed the opportunity to air some new views which I was working on at the time in the quiet of Cambridge's fine libraries. When eventually the University Press invited me to publish the lectures, I gladly welcomed the occasion to place them at the disposal of the wider reading public.

Certain themes of my Cambridge lectures I treated subsequently in Newcastle, Oxford, Paris and Tübingen, where I profited greatly from discussions with learned historians and lawyers, as I had done in Cambridge: for this I offer them my warmest thanks. My text has been expanded, brought up to date and annotated, but follows closely the original pattern of the four lectures as they were given in the spring of 1968.

R. C. van Caenegem
Ghent, July 1972

1

English courts from the Conqueror to Glanvill

'Ne inde clamorem audiam pro penuria recti'

It was with considerable trepidation that I undertook, as a continental scholar, to lecture on English legal history in an English
university, and particularly in Cambridge, where Maitland once
used to teach. Fortunately, I can plead extenuating circumstances
for this temerity, to which the Faculty in inviting me agreed, showing a commendable lack of prejudice. I have had the good fortune to
study in this country for a considerable time and to become familiar
with its history, notably by working on unpublished material in de-
positories large and small, up and down the country; above all I have
had the rare privilege of working on the early history of the
Common Law under the supervision of the late Professor T. F. T.
Plucknett, a very learned and patient master, who felt that a
continental approach to English history might throw some new
light on such questions as the possible Roman origin of certain
Common Law notions and procedures. Also, England is near to
my own country and their historical ties very close: the Flemish
knights and their retainers who joined William of Normandy
(married to the daughter of their own count) in the conquest of
England were numerous. Though this sort of military adventure is
now out of fashion, the intellectual adventure of conquering some
difficult problem of another country's history is equally thrilling.

One reason why my subject may be considered difficult, is the
state of the evidence. The contrast between the period from the
Conquest to Glanvill, with which I shall deal here, and the following
centuries is striking. Until Glanvill there were no comprehensive
law-books but only rather helpless attempts to state some rules of
law by authors who were clearly baffled by the diversity of English
customs and did not hesitate to incorporate rather indiscriminately
material from the Theodosian Code or the Salic and Ribuarian
Law.[1] There are no plea rolls, either central or local, none of those
curia regis, and assize rolls that begin to flow around 1200, so
many of which are now available in admirable editions; nor do we

1

dispose of the feet of fines before the reign of Richard I.[2] One also looks in vain for a stately series of legislative texts like the 'statutes of the realm' of a later age. The historian has to work with the miscellaneous mass of charters, conserved in original or in cartularies, which Henry VIII's policy scattered all over the country and where documents of judicial importance are *rari nantes* in the vast sea of humdrum donations and agreements. There are chronicles and letters which occasionally touch on law and law courts and scattered texts of final concords, in common use from the 1170s onwards and liable to contain data on procedure and court personnel.[3] A few royal enactments, such as Henry II's assizes, very informal texts (conserved because a chronicler has taken the trouble to include them) of an era when English kings were just beginning to relearn their rôle as legislators, have come down to us. The admirably edited pipe rolls, a solitary one for 1130 and a continuous series from 1156 onwards, are full of information for our subject (since royal justice had to be paid for) and unique in twelfth-century Europe. Not as explicit as we would wish, they leave a good deal in the dark that was not less important because it did not happen to pass through the administrative channels of the Exchequer. Above all, we have large numbers of royal writs, easy to trace for the period from William I to Stephen thanks to the three volumes of the *Regesta Regum Anglo-Normannorum*, but still unedited and even uncalendared as far as the English administration of Henry II is concerned.

When Glanvill wrote – for the sake of facility we shall thus call the author of the 'Treatise on the laws and customs of the realm of England commonly called Glanvill' – people were getting uneasy about unwritten laws. Customs might go unrecorded, but ought not royal legislation to be embedded in formal written texts, like the *leges* of the Roman emperors, which Europe was studying with great zeal and fascination in the *Codex* of Justinian? The texts of the assizes of Henry II tucked away in some monastic chronicle were very pale reflections of those imperial *constitutiones*. Glanvill mentions the problem and takes up a definite position. 'Although the laws of England are not written,' he says, 'it does not seem absurd to call them laws – those, that is, which are known to have been promulgated about problems settled in council on the advice of the magnates and with the supporting authority of the prince.' And he proceeds cleverly to turn the tables on possible Roman-inspired detractors of English laws by quoting from Roman Law to support his thesis: 'For,' he writes, 'this also is a law that "what pleases the prince has the force of law" and if merely for lack of writing, those unwritten laws were not deemed to be laws, then surely writing would seem to supply to written laws a force of greater authority than either the justice of him who decrees them or the reason of him who establishes them.' Glanvill, who must have been aware of the canonists' distrust of unwritten custom, then proceeds to prove *per absurdum* that it really is law, for, he writes: 'It is utterly impossible for the laws and legal rules of the realm to be wholly reduced to writing in our time, both because of the ignorance of the scribes and because of the confused multiplicity of those same laws and rules.'[a] He ends his Prologue by announcing his intention wisely to limit himself to expounding 'general rules frequently observed in the king's court'; thus he came to write the first, masterly exposition of the nascent Common Law of England – an enterprise that he rightly calls 'not presumptuous, but rather very useful for most people and highly necessary to aid the memory'.[b]

The subject of this study will be the formative years of the Common Law under the Anglo-Norman kings and the great Henry II, who added England to a long series of Angevin family acquisitions. By Glanvill's time, in A.D. 1187–9, the outline of this common law of England, administered by a cohesive body of justices and

[a] Ever since Gregory VII had sharply remarked 'Christ has not said "I am Custom", but he has said "I am Truth"', custom had been under a cloud of suspicion in leading ecclesiastical circles; thus Stephen of Tournai and Sicard of Cremona underlined Gratian's opinion that concessions to 'various customary laws, introduced because of the differences in time, temperament and place', should be restricted; they found local customs dangerous and preferred that the Church should be governed by laws, see G. Le Bras, Ch. Lefebvre and J. Rambaud, *L'âge classique, 1140–1378. Sources et théorie du droit*, Histoire du Droit et des Institutions de l'Eglise en Occident, vol. 7 (Paris, 1965), p. 215.

[b] G. D. G. Hall, *The treatise on the laws and customs of the realm of England commonly called Glanvill* (London, 1965), pp. 2–3. Glanvill's quotation of the maxim 'quod principi placuit, legis habet vigorem' (Inst. 1, 2, 6) is a whiff of romanism that has amazed F. Schulz, 'Bracton on Kingship', *English Historical Review*, 60 (1945), 171, to the extent that he declared it an interpolation – a most convenient way of dealing with texts that happen to stand in the way of one's particular vision of history – unfortunately, as Hall, p. 2, n. 1 remarks, 'the words are in all the manuscripts and Schulz's argument could be used to dispose of substantial parts of the treatise'.

3

following a distinct procedure, was clear and the basic elements established for many centuries. How the system described in the *Tractatus* originated, is what we have to examine. The importance of our subject needs little comment: the Common Law is one of the major legal systems of the world, and was also of great political importance. In the decisive seventeenth century the Common Law, that 'bulwark of individual liberties against what might well be called the irrepressible monarchic aspirations of kings',[4] was a potent weapon in the hands of Parliament, where the common lawyers were a formidable phalanx. But it is to the twelfth century that we must now turn our attention. In the first chapter I shall try to set the scene: we shall take a critical look at the state of the law and the courts and, above all, at the position of the monarchy. The second and third chapters will be devoted to writs as instruments for initiating procedure in the royal courts and to the jury, which became their ordinary mode of proof. Having seen how England acquired a comparatively modern common law, based on writs and recognitions, we shall ask in the fourth chapter why this modernization did not, as on the Continent, take the form of the 'infiltration' or the 'reception' of Roman law. In other words, having seen what did happen, we shall try to guess what might have occurred, and why it did not – a more profitable exercise than one might at first glance be inclined to believe.

The events of 1066 were a cataclysm of the first magnitude. They were much more than the mere accession of a new dynasty (not something new to the English) or even the massive dispossession and elimination of a native aristocracy: they created a split society, a country inhabited by two nations, the *Franci* and the *Anglici*, where a dominant minority introduced values, rules and a language different from those of the native masses. Led by the duke of Normandy, a band of knights accustomed to live in a feudal society, followed by clerics familiar with the latest papal ideas, came over from the Continent with a retinue of servants and traders and took over the kingdom of England, its churches and its landed wealth. They installed a military and quasi-colonial regime and covered the country with their proud, mighty castles and cathedrals. Eventually the country returned to a more normal state of affairs and the two nations and the two traditions amalgamated into one English country that was neither Anglo-Saxon nor Norman (nor Danish, nor

4

Flemish, to name two minority groups that left their marks in certain regions). It was ruled by an English king, lived under a common law, and spoke one language. The history of England between 1066 and Magna Carta can be written in terms of this conflict and the ensuing synthesis, of which the kings were the architects.

The amalgamation took place at the biological level, notably through intermarriage between Norman and English families. It was reflected in the disappearance at the end of the twelfth century of the traditional greeting 'to all lieges French and English' from the address of royal charters. In his treatise on the Exchequer (A.D. 1179) Richard fitz Neal, who was no dreamer, remarked expressly on this development. Talking of the murder-fine, he wrote: 'Nowadays, when English and Normans live close together and marry and give in marriage to each other, the nations are so mixed that it can scarcely be decided who is of English birth and who of Norman.'[5] He added, however, three little words of great weight: 'de liberis loquor' (I speak of free people). The qualification is important: the treasurer of England, who was also bishop of London, was only speaking, as he casually reminds his readers, of the people who count, and naturally left out the large anonymous majority of unfree villeins, who were born into their status and, as he remarks in the same breath, 'cannot alter their condition without the leave of their masters!' The qualification was superfluous for his contemporaries, but the official mind expressed it in so many words.

The amalgamation of the two nations can also, of course, be observed in the development of the English language, which after a massive absorption of French words emerged from the crucible of the Norman occupation as a very different tongue from that of Alfred the Great and Edward the Confessor. The same is true, and we shall dwell on this a little longer, in the field of military organization. In two solid books Professor Hollister has shown that Anglo-Saxon military institutions did not disappear because of the Norman introduction of a feudal defence system. Eventually a new army of mercenaries paid by the royal treasury, in which feudal became fiscal relations, was established; it was neither the *fyrd* of the Anglo-Saxons nor the feudal knight service of the Normans.[6] I have just used the word 'feudal' – quite naturally, as I was discussing military organization, because that is what feudalism was about. In so doing

5

I have unavoidably stepped into a hornets' nest. At least, though we must look at the issue and though much turns on a question of definition, I shall not offer 'my definition of feudalism'. I shall, instead, quote the biblical word 'by their fruits ye shall know them' and say this: when I see knights doing military service for the king, on expeditions or castle guard, because of the fiefs they hold – and there is little doubt that the *servitia debita* were introduced by the Conqueror – when I see barons, bishops and abbots do feudal homage for their lands and positions; when I see scutage paid on the knight's fee and statistics compiled of subinfeudation by royal vassals; when I see people holding their land 'in fee', and heirs paying reliefs for entering into their inheritances; when I see numerous quarrels and stipulations about reliefs and other 'feudal incidents', not least in the Great Charter itself; when I find the feudal rule of primogeniture and the equally feudal right of the wronged vassal to renounce his bond, the well known *diffidatio*; when I find the very feudal notion of 'felony' dominating the criminal law – when I see all those fruits of feudalism, then, I conclude that I am indeed faced with feudalism and the feudal state.

To deny English feudalism because it does not fit some pre-established restrictive definition will not help us. It is clear that 'English feudalism was a creation of the Norman Conquest'[7] and that Anglo-Norman England was a feudal state – 'the most perfectly feudal kingdom in the West'[8] – even if it does not pass the test of Mr Richardson and Professor Sayles. Those authors hold that 'for half a century or so from 1066 the English way of life was not sensibly altered' and that 'the structure of the state remained essentially as it was, modified perhaps, but not changed in any fundamental element, to accommodate any new ideas of the relationship between lord and vassal which the Normans brought with them'. After showing that English feudalism lost its original importance from the later twelfth century onwards, they conclude – not having forgotten to praise Freeman and to condemn Round, who 'had been a pupil of Stubbs' – as follows: 'The administration of medieval France can be termed feudal because sovereignty was divided between the king and his feudatories. If in this sense France was "feudal", England was not. If we call England "feudal", then we should find some other adjective to apply to France.'[9]

Two remarks are called for. First, it is true that from the later twelfth century onwards England quickly became a semi-bureau-

6

cratic state where feudalism lost its political, judicial and military significance and became restricted to the rules of land-holding and fiscal arrangements.[10] In this sense the very real 'first century of English feudalism' was also the last. Secondly, nothing justifies the equation of feudalism with 'divided sovereignty' within the state, i.e. political dismemberment. It was originally developed on the Continent by the Carolingians in order to secure cohesion and unity, through personal bonds of vassalage, coupled with the holding of land and offices of the king. The system played this rôle for some time in the realm of the Franks, in Anglo-Norman England and in the Norman kingdom of Sicily. The trouble with feudalism was that it depended entirely on the personal relation of the vassals with the king-feudal suzerain. If he weakened and failed to hold his vassals together, and they seceded followed by their own vassals, whole regions became independent and the kingdom disintegrated. This other face of feudalism was shown in France after the breakdown of Carolingian rule and in Germany after the collapse of the Staufen. Both situations, the centripetal and the centrifugal, are rooted in feudalism and nothing warrants our restricting feudalism to one of its faces only.

The disaster of Hastings and the introduction of continental feudalism caused a great and, it would seem, lasting trauma. The law introduced by the Normans was greatly abused in the seventeenth century, when the 'theory of the Norman yoke' was powerfully launched: the English had 'been in part disinherited of their free customs and laws by the Conqueror and his successors by violence and perjury'.[11] It led in the nineteenth century to controversy between Round and Freeman which still resounds in history books today. Perhaps the best therapy for a trauma is to explain it away. One has indeed the impression that some historians have indulged in this sort of exorcism. They argue on the one hand that nothing really changed after 1066 and on the other that everything was already present *in nuce* in the Anglo-Saxon kingdom; in other words they feel that the feudalism which the Normans brought with them was not real feudalism and that they did not really bring it, since the Anglo-Saxons already had something very similar anyway. The basis for this feeling may ultimately be a deep belief in continuity, such as led High Anglicans to believe that there was no breach of continuity between the medieval and the modern Church of England and that there had been no revolution in the

7

sixteenth century – a belief that led them, as Maitland put it, to hold that the Church of England 'had been protestant before the Reformation and Catholic afterwards'.[12]

Asking herself what was the peculiar characteristic of English feudalism, Miss Cam found the answer in its 'ultimate association with royal government', fruit of 'the marriage of feudalism with the non-feudal monarchic system that William the Conqueror inherited from Edward the Confessor'.[13] The marriage of Norman feudal leadership with Anglo-Saxon kingship is indeed the most striking example of the amalgamation of Anglo-Saxon and Norman strands: it made English kingship a very distinct phenomenon on the European scene. When William the Bastard was preparing his campaign, there were in Europe two kinds of rulers. On the one hand were the anointed monarchs, national kings, revered and distant figures like King Edgar, 'father of the monks', and the saintly King Edward the Confessor in England or Saint Henry II in Germany, quasi-episcopal 'rois thaumaturges', surrounded by a religious halo, who tended to be venerated rather than obeyed, respected rather than feared, distant father-figures closer to God than to the people, guarantors of justice and keepers of the immutable good old laws, secure in their hereditary dignity and the knowledge that royal blood flowed in their veins. On the other hand, particularly in anarchic France, were the territorial princes whose power was ultimately based on usurpation, violence and success in war and who ruled over small countries. They were tyrannical upstarts who made up through incessant and brutal personal intervention for their weak legitimacy and dealt in a high-handed way with people and situations which the law courts could not, or were not supposed, to face. They were feudal gang-leaders, not crowned heads, and such order as there was in their duchies and counties depended on their personal and iron-fisted intervention.

William of Normandy belonged very much to the latter type, which made the traditional ruler look very old-fashioned. He clearly was a son of the Norman race, who had, in the words of Professor Knowles, 'a drastic, hard directness, a metallic lustre of mind, highly coloured and without delicacy of shading, together with a fiery efficiency that easily became brutality'.[14] Having worked his way up from infancy through incessant battle, he established his rule and some form of feudal order upon the turbulence of Normandy, not least through his merciless cruelty. If he was respected, it was not because he was God's anointed, but because people who laughed at him were quickly taught a cruel lesson, like the unfortunate defenders of Alençon who waved hides and skins from their walls to taunt the duke with the fact that his mother's relatives were tanners – and suffered dreadful horrors after the capture of their town.[15] This man, who felt that the death penalty was too lenient and ordered blinding and emasculation instead,[16] conquered England through victory on the battlefield, as was his habit, and was crowned king, the ultimate achievement of a man of his rank. This violent ruler of a turbulent minor principality became the anointed of the Lord, the wealthy ruler of the best organized monarchy in all Europe. What he and his sons made of this unique chance shows the mettle of the dynasty. They rose to the occasion, realizing that the preservation of the old English tradition of kingship was all-important, as was the preservation of numerous other Anglo-Saxon institutions, not least the fiscal ones. The Conqueror did not, however, throw away the advantages of his position of feudal warlord in the Norman tradition: he stuck to what he knew, and continued to rule with an iron hand. What he looked like we do not know, for the famous description by the 'Anonymous of Caen' is largely a verbatim copy of Einhard's description of Charlemagne,[17] but that he was a master of statecraft we should not doubt: the exceptional strength of the English monarchy in his time stems largely from the combination, unique in Europe, of the immense prestige of Alfred the Great's and Edward the Confessor's sacred kingship with the iron strength and ruthless command of the Norman dukes.

No European country had a political organization comparable with England, least of all the illiterate duchy of Normandy. That region had undergone the disintegration of Frankish rule, and its Viking dukes laboriously built some order – using the feudalism that was then dominant in France – and restored some measure of monastic life by importing foreigners. There was no ducal chancery and no law books. The political form was personal rule and feudal allegiance – with all its consequent instability and arbitrariness. Fiscal organization was very primitive. Nor was Normandy a real fatherland for its knightly firebrands, but rather a stepping stone for further vast conquests. In England things were different. The country could be proud of a rich and ancient national culture, in which the vernacular – West Saxon having achieved a substantial

9

degree of uniformity – occupied a unique place. The royal chancery was, if modest in our eyes, a reality and was soon to become a model for the Continent.[18] The steady issue of royal writs was remarkable in quantity and for the regularity of the formulas; the use of the vernacular strengthened their national character and made for close contact with the population, their texts could be directly read out in the local courts to the assembled community – a unique feature at the time. No other monarchy disposed of the same means of direct, national taxation, nor were the interesting possibilities of frequent danegelds neglected by William and his successors. English coinage was technically superior and under complete royal control. Numerous boroughs had grown up as part of a deliberate royal policy for development and defence. Nowhere was the territorial organization so effective and the network of royal officers headed by royal sheriffs so uniformly established as in the English shires: there were no immunities or franchises after the continental fashion,[19] nor a fortiori any regional state-building. Nowhere was national unity so real or royal authority, that 'great tree with roots pushed into every pocket of soil that would nourish it',[20] so well established. Not in France, of course, where the Capetian king was little more than one territorial ruler among many others. He happened to hold sway over the Isle de France, the old duchy of France, as dynasties of counts held sway over Flanders, or Blois or – probably the worst brood of all – over Anjou. The old Frankish administrative divisions, the pagi, had disintegrated by the year 1000 and were replaced by fortuitous feudal châtellenies, clustered around some baronial castle. The kings of France disposed of no means of direct taxation even in their domaine direct, and certainly not in the whole of their kingdom. They had no chancery and, until about 1100,[21] issued no writs or mandamenta, as brevia were called on the Continent. So unusual was the request to King Philip I, on a visit to Poitiers in 1076, that he should seal a charter there, that he had to confess he had left his seal behind, not expecting to meet this sort of demand so far from home in a part of his kingdom where no king had been seen for ages.[22] Even if the German King/ Roman Emperor had preserved much more from the wreckage of Frankish kingship, his fiscal position was weak and he had to put up with the large autonomy of the Stammesherzogtümer and the danger of divided loyalties, if the pope ever claimed his rights over the bishops and abbots of the German Imperial Church. The

10

reason for this remarkable discrepancy is to be found in the disintegration of the Frankish Empire which had vastly overstretched its possibilities in pursuit of ambitious dreams of expansion and universal rule. Steering clear of the ghosts of dead empires – except in fancy titles – the English kings quietly and realistically went on with the organization of a purely national monarchy. They made the greatest progress at the very time when the disintegration of authority in France reached such extravagant proportions that the Church had to launch the movement of the Peace of God to secure the minimum of public order which kings and other rulers failed to provide; there was no need for this sort of arrangement in England, of course, nor was it ever introduced there,[c] as it was in France and Germany.

Yet, in contrasting England with Normandy we should refrain from exaggeration. We should remember that the old-English chancery was a modest affair and that Exchequer organization cannot be documented in Anglo-Saxon times,[23] while national unity had gone through some very bad moments until quite recently. All was not right in the English Church and legal and ethnic diversity was still very real. Moreover the Normans, although 'ignorant enough to despise the English'[24] and 'barbarians who were becoming conscious of their insufficiency',[25] had taken over or restored a good deal of the Carolingian inheritance and shown in Normandy, England and Sicily, a truly great gift for administration, statebuilding and law enforcement which left a lasting mark on the political development of Europe. Their dukes had kept in their hands more sovereignty – in judicial, monetary and military matters – than the typical French ruler of the time.[26] The Normans had, quite naturally, taken over and developed those realizations of the old-English kingdom that corresponded most with their own genius for domination and organization, while they drove underground other glories of old-English civilization, in religious life and vernacular literature, which they despised or distrusted. The appreciation of Norman and English merits varies greatly, and is liable to be even more subjective than most of our pronouncements on the

---

[c] See a slight qualification in F. M. Powicke, *The Loss of Normandy (1189–1204). Studies in the History of the Angevin Empire* (Manchester 1913), pp. 94–5, who quotes two very faint traces of the Truce of God in England, viz. in the customs of Chester and in the canons of the council of London A.D. 1142.

11

past. Maitland, not given to rash, sweeping statements, has written rather icily that 'it has not been proved to our satisfaction that the men who ruled England in the age before the Conquest were far-sighted: their work ended in a stupendous failure'.[27] If, as it might well be, the ultimate test of a state is safeguarding its people from foreign conquest, the old-English state was indeed a failure, but is it fair to judge a polity and a civilization by the accident of one – very narrow – military defeat?[d]

Rather than pursuing this controversial line, let us examine the state of the law courts, which did not, of course, escape the impact of Norman rule; and as the Common Law was and to a large, if diminishing, extent still is 'judge-made law', the importance of the history of judicial organization for our subject will be easily under-stood. The Norman impact opened a period of uncertainty. Customary law ruled supreme, since the remarkable and unique tradition of Anglo-Saxon dooms came to an abrupt end under the Normans, who knew no legislation at home, and practised it very little in England. Unwritten custom can be very uncertain and the co-existence of old and new social and ethnic groups with their re-spective customs was a setback for the legal unification that was in full force in the old-English state. William the Conqueror promised the English that they could keep their laws – but so could his continental followers. Old-English land law continued side by side with newly introduced feudal law. The old communal courts of hundreds and shires met beside the new feudal courts, where lords and vassals sat to judge and be judged. In the boroughs the old-English court met for the 'English' beside a quite separate borough court for the 'Frenchmen', who had arrived with the con-querors, lived according to their own customs and enjoyed their own privileges, notably some fiscal ones.

To make things even more complicated, William I decided to

---

[d] The 'Saxon–Norman conflict runs deep', and has done so for a long time. In more recent times Sir Frank Stenton did much to heighten our appre-ciation of the Anglo-Saxons generally, and Lady Stenton has stressed some of their legal and institutional achievements, whilst Richardson and Sayles have abused the Normans as if they were relatives of Bishop Stubbs. A spirited counter-attack was recently made by Brown, 'The Norman Conquest', pp. 109–30. It all depends on how one judges the effects of the Conquest and the anniversary year of 1966 brought forth a number of studies on this topic, too numerous to list here; for the older views we can consult D. C. Douglas, *The Norman Conquest and British Historians* (Glasgow, 1946).

12

introduce separate ecclesiastical courts, putting an end – at least in the hundred courts – to the Anglo-Saxon tradition of settling all disputes, even those involving churches and clerics, in common courts, where sheriffs, earls and bishops sat together. In a writ of 1072–6 he declared that the episcopal laws, which until then were not kept well or in accordance with the holy canons in the kingdom of the English, were to be emended. He ordained therefore that no bishop or archdeacon should henceforth plead in the hundred court concerning episcopal laws nor bring cases concerning the cure of souls before the judgment of laymen: whoever was summoned according to episcopal laws to answer on some cause or guilt should appear where the bishop told him and answer there and do what was right, not according to the [practice of the] hundred, but according to the canons and the episcopal laws, on pain of excommunication. Neither sheriff or other royal official nor any other layman was to meddle with the laws that pertained to the bishop, and justice was to be done in the episcopal see or where the bishop decided.[28] There was a welter of change. Nevertheless unaltered at the top stood the king and his magnates: the *witenagemot* before 1066 and the *curia regis* (i.e. the king and his feudal barons lay and ecclesiastical) thereafter. The latter remained for a long time as remote as the king and his *witan* had been.

Before long the Anglo-Norman kings added to the confusion with judicial innovations, i.e. the local justices and the justices in eyre. Although the former were a passing experiment they are of the highest interest, since they constituted a serious threat to the sheriff, that pillar of the old-English monarchy on the local level. The justices in eyre had a great future before them; as we shall come back to them later, all we need say here is that they definitely appear under Henry I. The *shire-gerefa*, the 'shire-reeve', is a well known and familiar figure, a precious Anglo-Saxon legacy, one of those 'good things' of the old-English monarchy which the new dynasty carefully preserved. The sheriff was the principal officer of the crown in the shire, collected the royal revenue there and conducted the judicial business of its court; the Norman kings gave the office to men of considerable importance, Normans of course, but managed to keep them firmly under control. The practice of the Exchequer shows that however big a man the sheriff was in his county, he was a trembling servant when he had to render account to his royal master. If we are on firm ground with the sheriff, the numerous *justiciae* and *justiciarii*, who appear in great quantity and often fleetingly in the firmament of twelfth-century England, are a different proposition. The term *justic'*, as it appears in the documents of the time, covers a multitude of rôles and capacities, from the *capitalis justiciarius* of the kingdom, holding vice-regal power, to obscure local justices who are mentioned once or twice in the address or the list of charter witnesses: everyone who had some authority could do justice – executive and judicial power went hand in hand. The Justiciar, the 'king's alter ego', was the head of the administration and in the frequent absences of the kings held vice-regal power. Some historians consider Roger of Salisbury in the time of Henry I as the first justiciar, others begin the series with Robert of Leicester and Richard de Lucy in the early years of Henry II's reign; however, the history of the office and its occupants is a well documented and well studied subject and need not further detain us here.[29]

We are not so well informed about the local justices. Royal officers appointed by the king to keep *placita coronae* and generally to look after royal interests in fiscal and criminal affairs in the local courts also came to handle a good deal of business in connection with royal writs. They were resident officials, introduced by Henry I, that great experimenter, and should not be confused with the justices in eyre or itinerant royal judges who appear around the same time and were called *justitiarii totius Angliae*, to indicate that their commission was supraregional. The local justices sitting in boroughs, hundreds and counties operated beside, and probably in competition with, the traditional sheriff. They were men of less exalted rank, very close to the king, who did not hesitate to raise talented men of low origin 'for their obsequious services'[30] and, unlike the sheriffs, not important local landowners. The office gained so much in prestige that under Stephen some very important people succeeded in laying their hands on it – Geoffrey de Mandeville, for example, and William de Roumare, earl of Lincoln, and successive bishops of Lincoln – and it reached its zenith in the early years of Henry II. It looked for a moment as if these royal justices might become the most important local judicial officers in the kingdom, to the detriment of the age-old shrieval function, much as the twelfth-century Flemish and French 'bailiffs' rose to the detriment of the old fashioned castellans and *prévôts*. But it did not happen. The local justices disappeared for good from the English scene, with surprising suddenness and with few exceptions, around 1166–8, evidently in connection with the rise of the itinerant justices.[31]

The old-English sheriff and shire did not disappear, as the Frankish *comites* and *pagi* had done in the turmoil of the tenth and eleventh centuries. The sheriff carried on, but in the judicial field he became a much less exalted figure, so that Professor Painter rightly speaks of an 'errand boy';[32] the rise of the central courts was not fatal to him as it was to the local justices, because unlike them he had many functions which could not normally and simply be taken over by the king's itinerant justices. However, that was a development of Henry II's reign; in the meantime the co-existence of several networks of courts and the experiments of Henry I with local and itinerant justices led to overlapping and uncertainty.

It was understandable that the Norman kings left the English their laws and courts, and also that they could not demand that their Norman followers should give up their feudal law courts; that they pressed for ecclesiastical courts for ecclesiastical affairs, as was common continental practice; and also that Henry I wanted to establish his own modern officers to deal specifically with crown pleas throughout the country, without abolishing the trusted immemorial machinery of shires and sheriffs. And it was, of course, natural that above all, the people had the remote but real possibility of obtaining a hearing in the *curia regis* itself, for which no rules of competency were devised. Some people and some cases certainly came before it – tenants in chief and state trials – while for others access to the curia was a question of connections and luck plus a bit of hard bargaining. But the inevitable result of it all was a good deal of overlapping, uncertainty and confusion. It was all right for the *Leges Henrici*[33] to say 'unusquisque per pares suos iudicandus est et ejusdem provincie', but if you were a cleric and someone's vassal, were you to go to the court of the county where you lived or to the court of the lord from whom you held your land and position or to the court of your bishop or your archdeacon (or, better still, were you to pay a solid sum into the royal exchequer or chamber to try and plead *in curia regis*)? Thus a writ of Henry I of 1108 sends to the county court suits on land between tenants of different lords,[34] whereas the *Leges Henrici* of 1114–18 sends a suit of this kind to the court of the lord of the defendant.[35] Although the writ of William I, mentioned above, forbade hundred courts to hold ecclesiastical pleas, it said nothing on shire courts, but as it

15

expressly forbade *leges episcopales* to be brought before laymen the shire courts should be excluded also. However, the *Leges Henrici*, the work of a man with practical legal knowledge, mentions ecclesiastical pleas as being the first to be examined in the shire courts, before the pleas of the crown and the rest.[36] Nor was it always easy to distinguish Church pleas; a special action had to be devised to decide by a jury of twelve lawful men whether a tenure was a knight's fee or a frankalmoin: if the latter, the case went to a Church court, if not, to a lay court; if the two parties claimed to hold of the same baron or bishop (acting here as a feudal lord and not as a prelate),[37] it went to his court, if not, to the king's court.[38] Nor did the universal laws of logic invariably apply: advowson, for example, being a complex of rights in a church and notably that of presenting a priest to the bishop for appointment to serve in it, would seem to be an obvious ecclesiastical cause, destined for the Church courts. And yet, it was declared a plea for the royal court in the Constitutions of Clarendon, even when the quarrel lay between clerics. Of course, it could be argued that advowson was part of the complex of rights of the landowner who had built the church for his villeins, but solid reasons to the contrary were not hard to find and had been applied in practice: so once again we see how uncertain the boundaries of court competency were.[39]

It is no wonder that many court records leave an impression of basic weakness, hesitation and slowness. We hear more of concords and settlements than of downright judgments of right or wrong. Nor should we forget how ineffective and inadequate some of the smaller courts were: quite possibly not enough suitors could be found or not one of them could read a Latin writ from the king, and if the clerk was ill, the activity of the court came to a halt.[40] And how was a minor local court to impose upon a reluctant powerful man the execution of its judgment, painfully obtained after the long delays of innumerable essoins were exhausted,[e] when some mighty barons tried even to disobey a royal command?[f] There can

[e] See payments in the pipe rolls made 'ut habeat terram suam sicut eam dirationavit' (31 Henry I, p. 11): it was not enough for Ranulf fitz Ingelran to have deraigned his land in the courts, he still paid 10 mark silver to get hold of it!

[f] King William I had given some Peterborough land to a household officer and he ordered, by a writ from Normandy, that the abbot should be given compensation, but the abbot refused, as we read in a Peterborough survey of c. 1100–c. 1110, see E. King, 'The Peterborough "Descriptio Militum" (Henry I)', *Eng. Hist. Rev.* 84 (1969), 97.

16

be little doubt that the judicial system in the first century after the Conquest went through a crisis, which was gradually worsened by uncertainties and doubts about the law of evidence, to which chapter 3 will be devoted. Miss Hurnard maintains that distrust of the ordinary courts led people who had committed a pardonable offence to ask rather for a royal pardon.[41] And as the uncertainties of court organization were paralleled by the uncertainties and multiplicity of the customs of various regions and classes, it is not surprising to find the king in his writs constantly ordering or forbidding something, 'so that I shall hear no further complaint for lack of justice'. *Penuria recti* or *defectus justicie* was clearly the evil of the age and the royal orders to do right 'without delay' show how slowly justice in the ordinary courts was enforced, if ever.

The author of the *Leges Henrici*, one of those poor law-books that mirror the perplexities of the age, was under no illusion. After writing that because of 'the perversity of the situation and the flood of evils, the definite truth of the law can seldom be found', he bitterly concludes his plaintive chapter 6 by saying that it is better 'to avoid claims and the utterly whimsical dice of pleas altogether'.[42] Modern authors find themselves in agreement with his black views, and speak of a 'quite inadequate judicial machinery'[43] and of local ministers of justice who were 'unequal to the task entrusted to them';[44] they find that 'in the early twelfth century men in England had every reason to be bewildered by the law'.[45]

What could wronged people do, if they decided to abstain from making their claim rather than risk the 'incerta penitus alea placitorum'? They could not turn to self-help, for violence was against the king's peace and sternly rebuked. If they were not prepared to let the matter rest, there was one great hope for them. They could obtain redress from the king's court itself, not the king and his barons meeting on great occasions of state, but the king and his permanent close collaborators. That is exactly what happened. In increasing numbers bewildered plaintiffs who had failed to find the right court, or to obtain judgment or its execution there, or who had not even tried the ordinary judicial way, attempted to find redress for their grievances by bringing their case before the king. This could be through an immediate royal order of restitution or a full judicial hearing in his court or through a writ to a local court ordering, with all the weight of royal power, that prompt justice

17

should be done. It was not surprising that people who despaired of the maze of feudal, communal and ecclesiastical courts and laws placed their hope in royal intervention. To the king – the fountain of justice – Englishmen and Normans alike could hopefully look. To the English he was the successor of their own old line of monarchs. William I had been hallowed in Westminster according to the ancient English rite by an English archbishop, Aldred of York, and Henry I had married Eadgyth, or Edith, a descendant of the royal house of Wessex. To the Normans he was a scion of their ducal house and their feudal overlord. The king held 'Englishmen' and 'Frenchmen' together. He was the mightiest man in the land, incomparably more powerful than any other man or family and even the Church was under his firm control. He was everybody's master and all land and the higher functions in Church and State were ultimately held from him.

English writers of the century of Henry I and Henry II are full of awe for the majesty of kings. The monarch is 'the likeness on earth of the divine majesty', the 'image of divinity'.[46] The *Leges Henrici Primi* talks of the 'tremendum regie maiestatis imperium'[47] and it is with the words *Regiam potestatem* that Glanvill opens his treatise, in a Prologue reminiscent of the Preface of Justinian's Institutes. The author of the Dialogue of the Exchequer was equally insistent on the eminent position of his master. Here too the opening words, *Ordinatis a Deo,* at once indicate in what key the work is composed. 'It is necessary,' says the royal treasurer, 'to be subject and obedient to the powers ordained of God with all fear, for all power is from the Lord God.' He then argues that it therefore cannot be wrong for ecclesiastics to serve kings, 'especially' – note the word – 'in those affairs which involve neither falsehood nor dishonour'.[48] And even if the wealth of kings is not theirs 'by strict process of law', and proceeds 'from their mere arbitrary power', 'their subjects have no right to question or condemn their actions'; they stand or fall by God's judgment and not man's.[49] *Vis et voluntas,* force and willpower were not lacking in the English kings of the time[50] and they were always ready to show it. The successors of the Conqueror had lost nothing of his iron determination: Henry I, the Lion of Justice, destroyed the false moneyers[51] and Henry II ordered the Inquest of Sheriffs and did not hesitate to dismiss them wholesale.[52] The king's word or his writ was to be obeyed by everyone as a matter of course and if this was not done at once, a second writ would express royal amazement and displeasure, impatiently enquire what caused the delay and tell the addressee to mend his ways at once:[53] contempt of a royal writ was a plea of the crown.

The outcome of it all, to which we now turn our attention, was the rise to absolute predominance of the central royal courts under Henry II, as the free man's courts of first instance for all the more important and frequent complaints connected with landholding throughout the country. There was a dual phenomenon here, centralization and specialization. Centralization meant that an enormous amount of litigation, that would in earlier times have originated in the local courts and stayed there, now came up before a central body of royal judges. The transfer of pleas from local courts through writs of *pone* and *tolt* was easily obtained and local courts were under constant central supervision through the rule *nemo tenetur respondere* (see pp. 25–7), the writ of prohibition[g] and the writ *de falso judicio*.[54] Under Henry I the enforcement of new royal enactments was left to the local courts.[55] Henry II entrusted this to his own justices in eyre. For a man who had unjustly lost his free tenement to appear in the *curia regis* was exceptional in A.D. 1100, but common by A.D. 1200. With centralization came professional specialization. The common nucleus of the central courts, i.e. of the justices in eyre, the Common Bench at Westminster, the Exchequer and the Bench *coram rege*, was the old feudal *curia regis*, something like the primeval amoeba in biology. In this undifferentiated body business of all sorts, political, fiscal and judicial, was transacted on non-professional, casual lines. Under pressure of work a division of labour developed. The barons of the Exchequer formed an institution, distinct, if not always separated from the king's justices;[56] among the latter some were justices itinerant, on eyre in the counties, others, of higher rank, resided at Westminster, still others, the Bench *coram rege* travelled with the king and could consult him if necessary. Initially these men had been temporarily borrowed from their other occupations. Later their work as royal justice became their main task. Their professional

---

[g] The writ of prohibition to court Christian was a royal writ forbidding a court Christian to proceed on a certain plea which was allegedly not within its competence. See G. B. Flahiff, 'The writ of prohibition to court Christian in the thirteenth century', *Medieval Studies*, 6 (1944), 261–313; 7 (1945), 229–90.

outlook and expertise improved correspondingly. They all formed one cohesive group, applied one common law and one set of procedures which was so conveniently expounded in Glanvill.

We are well informed about the rise of the body of central justices. It really began under Henry I when from the *curia regis* some *curiales* were sent on occasional eyres (=*itinera*, journeys) through a certain number of counties to hold pleas – mainly crown and forest pleas – and to supervise and supplement the work of the local courts. The country was not divided into circuits so as to be completely encompassed in these missions (unlike the later system of general eyres), and the itinerant justices were few – about a dozen for the reign of Henry I, with no more than about six at work at any one time[57] – but the essentials of the general eyre were there: a broad scope *ratione materiae* and officials sent *a latere regis* to *inter alia* judicial work on an eyre through several counties. There is nothing unique or amazing about this institution. The Carolingians had sent their *missi dominici* out, the Church knew episcopal visitations, the *curia regis* was itself constantly travelling around and doing judicial business, and even before Henry I's time the king had occasionally sent some trusted men to do justice in important causes in the country, although there had been no judicial eyres *ad omnia placita*. From the Pipe Roll of 1130 where we find such itinerant justices as Ralf Basset, Miles of Gloucester, Pain fitz John, Robert Arundel, Geoffrey de Clinton, Walter Espec, Eustace fitz John, Richard Basset, William d'Albini Brito and Aubrey de Vere we learn most of the system. The practice was obviously well established. It went under during the 'Anarchy', but was one of Henry I's experiments revived by Henry II, who was so keen to restore everything 'sicut fuit tempore avi mei' (as he often put it in his charters and writs). The revival did not come at once. The first years of the reign saw an occasional baron sent out on an eyre – Henry of Essex in southern England, Robert of Leicester in Buckinghamshire – but the general eyre reappeared in 1166, an important year in more than one respect, and from then onwards it developed far beyond anything known under Henry I. The general eyres which started again in 1166 were linked with the repression of felonies – the Assize of Clarendon – and measures to protect the possession of land – the (lost) Assize on Disseisin (see pp. 42–3) – beside the traditional forest pleas. While Alan de Neville was holding the latter in Worcestershire, Herefordshire, Stafford-

20

shire and Devon, Earl Geoffrey de Mandeville and Richard de
Lucy were sweeping through numerous counties from the south-
east to the north in quick tempo: by October this eyre was over.[58]
The year 1167 brought a pause. Geoffrey de Mandeville had died in
October 1166, but Alan de Neville continued on his forest eyre
and we can follow him in the pipe roll. In 1168 the general eyres
started again: this year saw the beginning of the systematic visita-
tion of the whole country, a permanent feature of English justice
for centuries to come. Activity – notably the enforcement of the
Assize of Clarendon – went on undiminished in 1169 and 1170 and
its geographical scope approximated to the comprehensive circuits
covering the whole country, which we find in 1176. Then, quite
abruptly, the Inquest of Sheriffs of 1170 brought everything to a
halt. Various political circumstances intervened (rebellion and
tallage in 1173–4) to interrupt the course of the general eyres till
1175. In that year they were back in full force, with two circuits,
one under Ranulf de Glanvill and Hugh de Cressi in the north,
and another under William de Lanvalei and Thomas Basset in the
south, while the king himself and several judges went on their own
iter. The years 1176 and 1177 witnessed important general eyres,
connected with the enforcement of the Assize of Northampton.
We find six groups, each counting three justices, who for the
first time were called *justicie errantes*. The eyre was clearly
becoming a regular machine for effecting a circuit of all the English
counties, although their composition still varied from eyre to eyre.
In 1178 the eyres were going on when the king came back from
Normandy in July and heard complaints about the excessive zeal
of his itinerant justices in enforcing the Assize of Northampton of
1176. He dismissed them and appointed instead five men to hear
complaints; they were to travel with him and to refer to him personally if need be. This measure seems to have been temporary and
can hardly be seen as the foundation of the Bench *coram rege*.
In the year 1179 after Easter there was a great council at Windsor
and the justices were sent out on eyres again, this time in four
groups, three of which were headed by bishops (not a very canonical
arrangement!); one of the four groups of justices travelled with the
king himself on the northern circuit. About this time the old, eminent
barons disappeared from the eyres and were replaced by lesser men.
In the 1180s the system worked regularly. On average we find some
twenty justices on eyre in the provinces; in 1189 they were thirty-

21

five, a considerable number that illustrates the progress since the eyres of Henry I.

In those years too the Bench of Common Pleas, a group of permanent royal justices sitting at Westminster, came into being. We do not know exactly when, but they were there when Glanvill wrote and their fixed seat at Westminster was one of the stipulations of Magna Carta. At Westminster the barons of the Exchequer where judicial business was sometimes done also sat. Above them all the king himself could intervene: when he was always absent, like Richard I, no regular court could develop before him, but when he was chiefly in the country, conditions were present for a Bench *coram rege*, i.e. a court of royal justices travelling with the king though not as a rule hearing cases in his presence. Thus the thirteenth-century Common Law courts had taken shape. The early years of the century saw the court *coram rege* become a permanent professional branch of the *curia regis*. Its competence vis-à-vis the Common Bench at Westminster is not easily defined, but it certainly included pleas that touched the king himself;[59] much also depended on the fortuitous presence of the king in a given part of the country. Both these courts ranked higher than the itinerant justices, although they all formed one body of 'justices of the lord king' applying one, common law. The general eyres remained important until the fourteenth century. Their business was twofold. They first dealt with pleas of the crown, on the basis of a list of questions known as 'the articles of the eyre', a miscellaneous collection of criminal and feudal affairs, and such questions as market control, treasure trove and the misconduct of officials. Then they also dealt with common pleas, ordinary litigation between ordinary parties, frequently under the possessory assizes and by royal writ – they take up most of the common pleas section of the eyre rolls – but not necessarily so. As these same cases could also be brought in Westminster, the question may be asked what or who decided which causes were to go where. The answer is that cases pending in the Common Pleas from the county affected were transferred to the eyre; in fact the Common Pleas started as an exceptional means of catering for those who would not wait for the next eyre. At a further stage the judicial function of the eyre was transferred to the Court of Common Pleas on the one hand, and to itinerant justices with restricted competence on the other (to hear possessory assizes, to deliver jails and, under *nisi prius*, to take from local juries verdicts in cases pending before the central courts). The general eyre fell into disuse.[60]

We know a good deal about Henry II's justices. What bound them together was the king's service. Some were powerful barons, but as time went on, men of simpler rank joined them. The former were rich in their own right, the latter became so by serving the king. Initially the king's household provided most of the justices, later other men with experience in royal service who had been sheriff, or had sat at the Exchequer or been keeper of a royal castle or bailiff of a royal manor were drawn in. For many this judicial work was only occasional. There were a considerable number of clerics, from bishops to simple clerks. Some were men with an academic background, enjoying the title of master, but they were a minority of about a dozen, not even ten per cent of the total force of justices between 1166 and 1189. Some had studied law in the universities, other justices had gained some acquaintance with Roman and Canon Law in a less extensive way: in general the training of a royal justice was very much a practical one. From service in the royal administration they worked their way up, learned the law and saw how justice was done. Initially they had to watch and listen. If they were lucky they found an older man who explained things at length, like the *magister* to the *discipulus* in the Dialogue of the Exchequer; at a later stage they had their lawbooks, where they could read it all.[61] They belonged in one way or another to the Norman upper class and French was for many centuries the technical language of the Common Law.[62] Rooted as they were in the feudal world of this class it is not surprising that feudal land law has been the core of the Common Law for centuries. These men, high powered professionals, were very different from the provincial suitors, lawmen and aldermen of the traditional local courts.

The process of centralization was not, of course, limited to law and law courts, or to England. It was a common development in the twelfth century, occurring in many spheres of life and many countries. In the Church an influx of litigation from all over Latin Christendom created problems. Through appeal or otherwise, masses of litigation were already coming before the papal curia by the middle of the century. Nothing, not even the high cost of pleading, would stop parties rushing to Rome. The curia could not possibly deal with them all and resorted to papal judges delegate. This

23

solution, a very common feature of the century, combined the advantages of local examination and a hearing by people who knew the country and its ways, with those of an inquest and judgment by judges who were not the ordinary local ones, who carried all the weight of papal authority and would apply the best procedure available. But the use of papal judges delegate was only a brief phase before a long-term solution was found with the gradual establishment, from the late twelfth century onwards, of episcopal officialities. They formed a complete network of local Church courts, staffed by learned and professional judges and applying the modern canon law taught in the universities. They were streamlined by the facility of appealing along the hierarchical ladder, from the bishop's officiality to the archbishop's, and finally to the pope. The papal solution stands out clearly: one canon law, developed by the international corporation of scholars and the popes, supreme legislators and judges; and one hierarchical and centrally controlled net of episcopal and archiepiscopal courts, with the Roman curia at the apex. Towards the middle of the thirteenth century the French solution was established: here we find a network of local courts under royal *baillis* and *sénéchaux*, supervised by the Parliament of Paris through the possibility of appeal and evocation. The situation was similar to that of the Church, from which the procedure of the Paris Parliament was borrowed, but French law was far from showing the unity of canon law – and would, in fact, never do so before the end of the Ancien Régime. Seen in this light the English solution is an interesting variety. It created one very large central court of first instance for the whole country, consisting of the king and his justices and operating in two sections: one was immobile and sat at Westminster, the other mobile and travelled all over the country, bringing the justice of the king's court right to people's door-steps. They encompassed town as well as countryside, for boroughs were expected to send twelve men to meet the justices when they came round. They all applied one and the same common law of England.

In the face of this overpowering display of central justice, the old local courts – in the baronial honors, counties and boroughs – sank into the comparative insignificance in which they have remained for many centuries. Even today, after the creation of the county courts in 1846 and the Judicature Acts of 1873 and 1875, English judicial organization astounds the continental observer by its highly

24

centralized nature. The form of centralization adopted in England was the outcome of many experiments and contradictions. The central justices did not have the local roots of the sheriffs and local justices of Henry I's time, but they were not permanently shut up in a remote hall in Westminster. They were royal officials, not regional magnates commanding a network of feudal courts. Their law concerned all free men of the kingdom of England, whether English or Norman, and all free tenures, whether feudal *stricto sensu,* such as knight's fees, or not, such as tenure in socage or burgage. Centralization – and concomitant specialization – created its own problems. By putting litigation into the hands of a professional body the king created an institution, which – according to one of the laws of the species – developed its own ways and traditions and tended to escape royal supervision: it was the guardian of 'custom and justice' against 'will and violence', even the king's. This contradicted the monarchy's principle of personal rule and we see, therefore, that while the kings gave away business with one hand to various central offices of state, they kept with the other the possibility of by-passing and overriding these great *corps constitués* and dealing personally and freely with such business as they chose. No government is possible if everything is in the hands of traditional departments and their routine, and certainly no system of personal rule can survive or accept such a state of affairs. The possibility must remain open to the ruler to deal personally and quickly with certain affairs, short-circuiting the great institutions. I quote as examples the Chamber and the Wardrobe as opposed to the Exchequer, the secretariat with the privy seal as against the chancery with the great seal, the Common Bench as against the Bench *coram rege.*

Centralization also meant central control over the activity of local courts. There is no need here to go into such ordinary devices as evocation of pleas or attacks on false judgments and verdicts. But there was one peculiar phenomenon that deserves our attention. We read in Glanvill that 'no one was bound to answer concerning any free tenement of his in the court of his lord unless there was a writ from the king or his chief justice'.[63] The rule *nemo tenetur responderé* meant that the king controlled access to the courts of his barons, for it was plainly useless to start an action there unless one obtained first a writ of right, i.e. a royal order to the court to do full justice, without delay, to the party named, on the complaint

25

specified.[64] That vassals could not plead in their lord's court if they so wished was a remarkable restriction, unknown even in Normandy, where development was so similar to that in England. That this royal restriction only arose in England, where feudalism was kept in royal hands as nowhere else, is striking but understandable. But how and when did it arise? Clearly not before pleading by writ of right had become current. Bringing a claim in a local court *per breve domini regis*, i.e. backed by a royal order 'to do right', was a well known device to impress a local court in Henry I's day; not only do we have writs on those lines but we find in the Pipe Roll of 31 Henry I various payments 'to have right concerning one's land' which suggests royal intervention, and we know that courts were well advised to take due notice, for royal displeasure and crushing amercements were the last thing anyone in twelfth-century England wanted to incur. A royal habit of safeguarding people and churches against (wanton) impleading, by granting the privilege that they could not be brought to court unless at the king's special command was also developing. Again in the Pipe Roll of 31 Henry I we find people paying so that they shall not have to answer the claim brought against them – it was the king who opened or shut the gate of justice.

Royal control over pleading in local courts took various forms. Early in Henry II's reign, not later than 1158, the term *breve de recto* appears and the advantage of bringing an action in a local court supported by a royal 'writ of right' was so obvious that it became a current practice. One of the *causes célèbres* of the time was the case of Richard d'Anesty, who carefully wrote down what it cost him. The first thing we read is that he 'began by sending one of his men to Normandy to obtain a royal writ by which he impleaded his adversaries' (A.D. 1158).[65] This was the way for well advised people to open a suit. In the Middle Ages when 'the transition between practice and custom was usually brief'[66] such a usage turned easily into a customary rule. Ten years or two precedents were according to several learned authors long enough to establish a custom.[67] A customary rule *nemo tenetur respondere* is to my mind very acceptable in the given circumstances. The other possibility, favoured by Lady Stenton, is that the rule was of legislative origin and in fact introduced by an enactment of Henry II.[68] There is no inherent impossibility or even improbability in this view and the fact that no text of this supposed assize has survived is no

26

argument against it: other 'assizes' and 'statutes' have been lost and kings could even proclaim new rules by word of mouth.[69] A more serious objection is the fact that nobody has even alluded to this supposed enactment. What, however, I think carries much more weight is the express and unambiguous statement – not an 'opinion' – of Glanvill that the rule is of customary origin.[70] I cannot imagine that Glanvill, who writes at length about customs and royal enactments, could here have confused them, nor that Glanvill would not have heard of an assize of that importance made by his own master, nor why he should want to mislead his own readers: when he expounds a rule that is of legislative origin he says so clearly enough.[71] The combined weight of Glanvill's definite statement, its instrinsic probability and the absence of any argument or text against it, amount to a very strong case. Could it be that Lady Stenton, who does not believe in a great Norman contribution, pleads so vigorously against it because a customary rule points towards an evolutionary development, going back to the Norman period? But then, even Anglo-Saxon kings were known to send injunctions to local courts to treat certain cases as specially interesting to the crown.[72]

Some authors have been shocked by the tyrannical nature of this rule, since it barred the way to the courts to ordinary litigants, except with the goodwill of the king. Apart from the fact that un-checked wanton impleading could easily become a tyranny of a different sort, especially in an age of inordinate thirst for litigation, the rule protected people who were in seisin – one of the most con-spicuous royal preoccupations. Further, the writ of right quickly developed into a writ *de cursu*, i.e. delivered as a matter of course on demand and against payment of a reasonable customary fee.[h] In 1177 already we find half a mark or 6*s.* 8*d.* being paid *pro brevi de recto*, which is a small sum compared with the average baronial revenue calculated for the period 1160–1220 at £202 (the median income at £115), or with the annual income of £10 to £20 required to support a man as a knight (the Assize of Arms of 1181 suggests 16 marks a year as the minimum income for a knight). The mini-mum fee set by Richard I to be paid for the pleasure of participating

[h] The notion of the writ of course can easily be older than the first appear-ance of the technical term on the records, i.e. A.D. 1200. It seems doubtful that the writ of right was issued free from the start, even for land of small value, but see Stenton, *English Justice*, p. 30.

in tournaments was 4 marks, for a landed knight.[73] Half a mark was the minimum below which amercements in the king's court did not fall.[74] This certainly took away the tyrannical edge which the rule would have had if the granting of the writ of right had been an arbitrary and expensive privilege.[75]

Thus it appears again that the rise of centralized justice and the shaping, if not the creation, of a common law came about not by one stroke of genius, a solemn enactment creating a new law court and a new set of rules devised by a group of learned lawyers and provident statesmen, but gradually and along some surprising roads and paths, which are as baffling to the logician as they are delightful to the historian. But more will be said about this in the following chapter.

2

Royal writs and writ procedure

'Praecipio ut juste resaisias'

About A.D. 1200 the main features of the Common Law and the central courts were fixed for many centuries. England would have one national law and not a multitude of local and regional customs; one corps of royal justices, whether sitting at Westminster or travelling in the counties, to administer and develop it; and not Roman or canon but feudal law as its core. It was also clear that the procedure would be by writ, which meant that in order to have access to these courts the complaint had to fit into one of the existing forms of action, i.e. the original writs. The technical term *breve originale* for a royal commission to try a case, originating judicial proceedings appears in 1203.[1] The original writs issued from the Chancery. Another great class of Common Law writs, the judicial writs, issued from the courts and concerned various other steps and measures connected with litigation. Original writs specified the nature of the complaint, the names of the parties, the object of the plea and other elements concerning summons, impanelling of juries and so on.

These forms of action, collected in the Register of Writs, and real keys to the king's courts, were limited in number, although they could be increased by the Chancellor to meet the demands of legal development. Each governed a separate and distinct procedure, with a particular time limit for bringing the action, specific modes of proof, summons, essoins and means of enforcing judgment, varying according to the circumstances and ideas at the moment of its creation. Each was devised for a particular grievance, for the idea – or shall we say the fiction? – was that access to the royal courts was limited and exceptional and that the local courts were and remained the ordinary courts of law for the country at large.

All this reminds one of the formulary system in classical Rome and the praetor creating new formulae,[2] although one should keep in mind that in England the judges kept strict control over new writs and did not hesitate to quash them on legal grounds,[3] whereas the Roman judge could not reject a formula given by the praetor.

The clerks of the Chancery, who wrote hundreds of the various types of Common Law writs, must quickly have felt the need for a formulary, from which to copy the stereotyped phrases. This also acquired legal significance, for no understanding of the Common Law and its procedure was possible without knowledge of its writs, both original and judicial.

Thus the Register of Writs came into being. The oldest surviving specimens are from the 1220s. New writs were devised as the law developed and were added to the Register. Between these oldest copies and the first printed Register of 1531 the number of writs was vastly expanded.[4] An official 'master Register' was most probably kept at the Chancery,[5] though no copy has survived, and numerous unofficial registers circulated in private hands throughout the country, together with other material which landowners found useful in waging their legal battles. It can be argued that a Register of Writs, at first possibly in the form of strips of writs kept in a fixed sequence, was already in use in the twelfth century.[6] The number of stereotyped writs in use at the time was already considerable, as we see in Glanvill – in a way our first formulary of writs as well as our first treatise on the Common Law.

The term 'writ' is very vague. It can mean any writing, even a book, as in 'Holy Writ'. More specifically, it was a brief official written document (Lat.: *breve*) ordering, forbidding or notifying something. It differed from a charter or diploma – a much older diplomatic form – because it was not so formal, solemn and detailed. Nor was it primarily conceived as a title deed, although it could fulfil that rôle. When Anglo-Saxon kings made or confirmed a grant they could notify a local court; initially this was done by word of mouth, but when this oral message was replaced by a written notification, authenticated by a royal seal, this document, although essentially still a communication to a local court or community, could serve as a title deed for the beneficiary instead of the traditional charters. Unlike the latter, the writs were not authenticated by a series of subscribers' and witnesses' names and crosses, but by a royal seal, appended *sur simple queue*, i.e. on a tongue cut from the bottom of the parchment so as to leave a step at the left, a technique that was new to Europe. Writs were also distinctive because they were written in the vernacular, at least until the coming of the Normans.

The royal writ as an administrative and legal instrument was a very important creation of the Anglo-Saxon monarchy; it was taken over and developed by the Norman kings, who knew nothing of the kind at home. There is no doubt that the familiar writ of Norman and Angevin times had been used by English rulers since the tenth century at the latest. The oldest surviving texts of royal writs go back to the reign of King Æthelred II (A.D. 978–1016),[7] the oldest surviving originals to Edward the Confessor.[8] Progress in regular administration was so great in tenth-century England that the use of this comparatively sophisticated device comes as no surprise.[9] Miss Harmer, to whom we owe an admirable edition of the Anglo-Saxon writs, has argued that they were already in use in the time of King Alfred. The learned author quotes a passage inserted by King Alfred into a translation of St Augustine's *Solilo-quies* mentioning the case of a lord's *ærendgewrit* and his *insegel* being brought to a man.[10] Dr Harmer took this as a clear reference to the sealed writ, as we later know it, but Dr Chaplais has argued recently that this is not necessarily so: the parchment and the seal may well have been separate. Sending a message – oral or written – and handing the messenger a seal for authentication was not an unknown practice.[11] Some doubt therefore remains as to the possible use of royal writs in Alfred's time, although it is clear that a written royal message despatched together with a royal seal was, of course, very close to it.

The great majority of surviving old-English writs are notifications of grants which could serve as title deeds and can therefore be called writ-charters, as opposed to the writ-mandates. But that was certainly not their only function. Among them are royal orders to perform certain tasks – temporary commands as opposed to lasting grants, administrative or judicial orders as opposed to title deeds. Naturally these ephemeral texts have survived in very small numbers since there was no incentive to conserve them. Even Dr Chaplais, who seems to consider the Anglo-Saxon writ to be really a writ-charter,[12] admits that Æthelred II 'occasionally issued administrative orders in writing, and that these written orders were accompanied by a seal', and he refers to the *gewrit and his insegl* sent by the king to Archbishop Ælfric of Canterbury, ordering him and the thegns of East and West Kent to settle a disputed claim to land at Snodland (A.D. *c.* 995).[13] This sort of written order should not unduly surprise us. I described in the previous chapter (p. 27, n. 72) how Æthelred II in 990–2 commanded orally, through a

31

messenger carrying a royal seal, that a case between Wynflæd and Leofwine should be settled as justly as possible. It was quite natural that as oral notifications developed into written ones this type of order should also have been put in writing.

We know that in the Kingdom of the Franks ephemeral written orders and notifications – the *mandamenta, indiculi, jussiones* – co-existed with solemn royal title deeds – the *praecepta*. Those Frankish *indiculi* are known to us almost exclusively thanks to official and private formularies, since their temporary character made conservation of the actual documents pointless. It is tempting to see in them the model of the Anglo-Saxon writs, which developed into remarkable instruments of government in England at the very moment, the tenth and eleventh centuries, when they disappeared on the Continent together with the Carolingian state. However, the formal dissimilarities between *indiculus* and writ make it highly probable that the latter is an original product.[14] The Norman kings, always quick to recognize and conserve good methods of government, continued and expanded the use of writs in a great variety of circumstances – but using Latin instead of English – and their writs have come to us from the twelfth century in their hundreds. They were routine documents and their crisp style, authoritarian tone and precise, economical wording, reflecting the masterful attitude of the rulers, make them a striking feature of the age, notably in the Common Law process, to which I shall refer later. It is not surprising that they served as models for the *mandamenta* sealed *sur simple queue* on the Continent from the end of the eleventh century onwards, in the wake of a general progress of political and administrative reorganization.[15]

The writ process, as it flourished around 1200, was not introduced ready made by some enactment, as St Louis introduced the Romano-canonical procedure in France around the middle of the thirteenth century, or the Emperor Maximilian in Germany at the foundation of the *Reichskammergericht* in 1495. There was no decree promulgating a *Code Civil* and a *Code de Procédure Civile* as happened on the Continent in the nineteenth century, or introducing socialist law and procedure as happened in various countries in the twentieth. The writ process grew historically and even haphazardly and was certainly not planned and conceived initially as a new system of law and law courts destined to supersede local courts and customs, although eventually that is what happened.

It is difficult to be certain when people first noticed that a new system had actually risen in their midst. The twelfth century was one of these epochs when everything was questioned and any number of new roads might be taken with effects which would last for centuries. It is not because people make momentous decisions that they are conscious of their importance and scope: many important steps are taken on the spur of the moment when 'provisional' measures have to be taken to fit new circumstances. By the time of Glanvill's *Tractatus*, at the end of Henry's reign, it was, of course, clear that the law and the courts had gone through a fundamental change, but at what moment in the course of that reign, so rich in inventions and adaptations, this was first perceived it is impossible to tell. By the time a new trend or practice hardens into a new system or institution and is seen as such, people can seldom remember how it all started. The new Common Law had originated through a number of unconnected or very loosely connected remedies, processes and initiatives, devised for the protection of various interests and the redress of the different forms of injustice that plagued society most and needed most urgent attention. To have grasped and described systematically these writs and forms of action as a whole, including a fair amount of substantive law too, was Glanvill's great merit.

It is with the earliest history of those writs and forms of action that we shall now be concerned. And here two points are essential. First, the rise of the central courts and of the Common Law they administered was not the result of a deliberate and frontal attack by the kings on the local courts, whether they were Norman feudal courts or Anglo-Saxon hundred and county courts; in fact those courts were by-passed and outflanked by the more modern and efficient protection offered by the central courts. The old courts were not legally stripped of their competence, but the alternative offered by the royal justices was so much better than anything the antiquated and archaic process of the local courts could offer that the royal courts were bound to attract litigants from all over the country. Yet legally speaking there was nothing to stop a plaintiff from obtaining an old fashioned writ of right and bringing his action in a local court rather than obtaining redress in the king's court; but then nobody who would rather use a torch or an oil lamp, as in the good old days, is obliged to light his house by electricity now. And the second point is this. The historical

33

origin of the Common Law writs, by which full judicial proceedings were started, is to be found in the executive writs of the Anglo-Norman kings, ordering redress of injustice by way of peremptory commands of reseisin or restitution, as a police measure and after the merest enquiry into the merits of the case: there was the minimum of procedure and the maximum of expediency. Judicialization turned these executive measures into original writs and judicial instruments initiating formal lawsuits only at a later stage; this was done piecemeal, each new type of writ commanding a specific form of process, so that a good deal of procedural variety resulted.

The starting point was the irrepressible urge of plaintiffs to rush to the king instead of trying the local courts. In England as in France, where the popular saying is documented,[16] people must have felt that 'wherever the king was, there was the law'. The sorry state of the traditional courts and the contrasting power and prestige of royal majesty, combined with Norman toughness, explain why people resorted to royal *vis et voluntas* rather than to *judicium*,[a] and preferred *jus regium*[17] to the old customs. What has been said about the papal *curia* of the time applies equally to the king's court: business grew, not primarily because the kings desired it, but because litigants could satisfy their own purposes better at the royal court[18] in a century of extraordinary 'litigious thirst'.[19] If you had been disseised, i.e. dispossessed of some land, because your neighbour annexed it and ploughed it or sent his cattle or his servants in and reaped your harvest;[20] or if your lord refused to give you seisin of the land of your deceased father and deprived you of your inheritance; or if your serfs ran away or were enticed away, allured by another lord or the liberating air of the towns, and you were lucky enough to know somebody at the royal court and wise enough not to forget that there were such things as the Exchequer and the Chamber and that kings were usually in financial straits and not inclined to act for nothing – you might obtain a royal

---

[a] Hugh the Chantor in his *History of the Church of York*, ed. C. Johnson (London, 1961), p. 29 reports a statement by bishop Herbert of Norwich, drawing a very sharp contrast between acts done according to a judicial sentence and those merely ordered and willed by the king, in the following words: 'non iudicio, set iussu regis et voluntate'; or, as the bishop of Durham put it: 'non iudicamento, set voluntate regis et imperio' (the author is speaking of the profession of subjection made by the new Archbishop Thomas of York to the see of Canterbury, A.D. 1109).

34

hearing. After the necessary explanations about your good right and the inadequacy of the local courts and your reason for fearing or mistrusting them and your firm confidence in the king as fountain of justice, a royal writ might be drafted and sealed in your favour. Disobeying it was a plea of the crown, a very serious matter. The writ might be an order to the local court quickly and fully to deal with your complaint, so as to satisfy justice and the king, who had shown his interest in the case – here we recognize the writ of right (*breve de recto*) of the Common Law, containing a clause for the removal of the case if the court failed to do its duty. Better still, you might obtain a writ addressed to the culprit or to the sheriff ordering him to see to it that you were at once given what had been taken or withheld from you.

Such royal orders, or executive writs, were in line with the prevailing attitude of the Anglo-Norman kings and had obvious advantages as means of restoring law and order quickly and forcefully. A royal order was not something to overlook with impunity. Their tone is unmistakable and left no room for dithering.[21] The detailed account in the Abingdon Chronicle of the dispute between the abbey and Turstin, son of Simon, the first case of Henry II in Bigelow's *Placita*, throws interesting light on such royal intervention (one hesitates to call it justice). Under King Stephen Abbot Ingulf disseised Walter fitz Hingam, who had failed to pay his due, of some property and took it into his own hand. Although according to the chronicler this was a normal step against a defaulting tenant, the disseised knight and his father in law, Simon, who had transferred the manor to him, took it very badly. In 1153 Turstin, son of Simon, went to the king and accused the abbot of having occupied, unjustly, land that belonged to him by hereditary right. He gave gifts to the king to obtain restitution and thereupon, according to the Abingdon story, the king ordered by his writ that, without delay, Turstin was to be reseised of the land. This came as a grave shock to the abbot, who was not inclined easily to comply with Stephen's peremptory order and convened his court to see what could be done. There were postponements and Turstin, seeing that his case was making no progress, decided not to appear in the abbot's court and to go to the king instead. He told the king (a lie, according to the chronicler) that the abbot refused to comply with the royal order of reseisin and he did not forget to make donations to the king and his entourage. The king was convinced of Turstin's

35

good right and ordered the sheriff of Berkshire, Henry of Oxford, to deal with the case 'ablato omni dilationis scrupulo' and 'secundum jus regium', possibly because contempt of a royal writ was involved. This meant the end of hesitation and postponement: the sheriff, 'rege jubente', gave seisin to the plaintiff thereby 'robbing the just possessors', according to the chronicler, who adds that the sheriff was 'depraved by love of money' and confessed later that he acted unjustly. In that same year King Stephen died and was succeeded by Henry II. Now it was the monks' turn to rush to the king and gain his ear. They were successful – the chronicler mentions no donations this time – and as the king saw their case to be just, he sent two successive writs ordering the case to be tried in the county court of Berkshire, where the abbey was situated. This time it was Turstin's turn to procrastinate, alleging various excuses for two years. Whereupon the abbot went again to the king imploring final satisfaction. The king was agreeable, assembled several members of his court and ordered them to try the case between the abbot and Turstin, who had also turned up, sensing that the dénouement was near. The court felt in favour of the abbot but dared not take it upon itself to disseise Turstin of the property unless the king himself gave judgment in that sense. Judgment was then given in favour of the abbot.[22]

It was in this way that 'arbitrary, even irresponsible interventions in law suits' took place. It may be true that 'in just this way royal justice began to be made more widely available',[23] but the disadvantages were glaring. Judicial proceedings are, of course, slow, because they go deeply into the matter, both sides are heard, documents inspected, experts consulted, witnesses or jurors come forward and procedural rules must be observed. Purely executive redress, which 'envisaged no trial, prejudged the issue and authorised reseisin without further preliminaries',[24] in sum direct police action, is quick but it is a hit-or-miss technique. It is ill-informed, one-sided and arbitrary and leads to injustice and contradictory, self-defeating measures. In the end it causes even greater wrongs than it sets out to combat.

Kings could be misinformed and there were people who lied to the king – and were amerced when found out[25] – or kept silent about some important point.[26] It was not impossible to make kings believe something which they afterwards had to retract. Thus the manor of Wrabness was – temporarily – lost to the abbey of Bury

36

St Edmunds because Henry I 'had been led to believe' by Richard fitz Walchelin that the manor did not belong to the demesne of the abbey – all this the king made clear with disarming simplicity in his writ of restoration, addressed to 'the bishop of London and the bishop of Norwich and Aubrey de Ver and Robert fitz Walter and all his barons and lieges, French and English, of Essex and Norfolk and Suffolk and all the barons and men of the honour of the abbey of St. Edmunds'.[b] Since the kings were capable of giving away 'inadvertently' – and admitting their errors openly – churches that did not even belong to them, it is hardly surprising that their interventions for the sake of justice were liable to go utterly wrong.[27]

People began to obtain writs to be safeguarded against other, possibly disadvantageous writs. Such a writ to defeat other writs – from the same royal source – was addressed by Henry I to the abbot of Ramsey, forbidding him 'to do Hugh Oilard anything but right, no matter what writ might be produced'[28] and the same king forbade, for the benefit of the abbot and monks of Gloucester, their having to plead concerning the land which Roger of Bayeux held of Archbishop Thomas of York in the manor of St Peter of Standish 'for any writ or order' that might be issued.[29] Richard d'Anesty, the hero of a famous lawsuit, whom we met in chapter 1, knew all about waging his little war of writs: no sooner had he heard that his opponents were hoping to obtain a writ to delay the plea than he sent his brother to the king overseas in order to obtain a writ to the effect that the plea should not be delayed because of a possible writ obtained by his adversaries to the contrary effect.[30] In such circumstances, contradictions and errors were unavoidable, nor were they limited to the state. Ecclesiastical dignitaries found

[b] Van Caenegem, *Writs*, nr 15, p. 419, A.D. 1128(?). The writ adds to the order of restitution that if the son of Richard wants to argue that Wrabness used not to be of the demesne of the abbey, the abbot shall hear the case in his court and do right thereof. The Pipe Roll of 31 Henry I, p. 96, reveals that the king's 'confession' and his order of 'restitution' were not obtained for nothing, since we find there that the abbot of St Edmund's Bury rendered account for 25 marks of silver for retaining *manerium quod dederat Ric' fil' Walchelin'*, an entry that throws a sinister sidelight on the dealings between the king and the abbot. There is a writ of King Stephen confirming Wrabness to the abbey 'finaliter imperpetuum solutum et quietum ab omni calumpnia ad victum monachorum, ita ne amplius respondeant inde Rogero filio Ricardi filii Walchelini neque heredibus suis neque alicui aliter qui quicquam inde clamet *pro aliquo brevi quod veniat*': it was a war not of words, but of writs! (*Regesta Regum Anglo-Normannorum*, III, nr 769, p. 283, *anno* 1135–48).

themselves in the same predicament. We see Abbot Walter of Arrouaise notifying the bishop of Bath and other persons that, having been misinformed, he has sent letters to Harrold Priory to the effect that Missenden Abbey had obtained a false charter from the pope by misrepresentation; he now acquits the abbey of the charge, cancels his letters and orders the priory to be obedient to Missenden.[31] We find Bishop Henry of Winchester revoking the award of the church of Sopley to the canons of Breamore made 'out of ignorance', since it really belonged to the canons of Christ Church, Twynham.[32]

Papal government did not avoid the pitfalls of erroneous orders of redress[33] given on the basis of one-sided information, the 'natural outcome of a supreme authority dependent on ex parte statements'.[34] Several examples concerning English cases occur in Professor Holtzmann's collection. From a letter of Urban III it appears that some people had got into the Hospital of St Peter in York on the strength of papal letters of recommendation, obtained under false pretences, i.e. having hidden the fact that they were monks who had left their monastery.[35] In a letter of Celestine III we hear of a cleric, Simon of Hailes, who had fraudulently obtained papal letters by hiding the fact that judgment had already been given against him.[36] A letter of Alexander III of 1181 for Christ Church Canterbury admits that previous orders of the same pope had been obtained 'falsa suggestione'. Therefore says the pope, 'if we have written to you on the false suggestion of some people, you are not held to obey our order on that point'[37] – so it was left to addressees of papal mandates to decide whether the pope had not acted on 'false suggestions' of their opponents, an extraordinary state of affairs! The war of contradictory orders was no royal monopoly: in a letter of 1176 Alexander III told Archbishop Richard of Canterbury to take no notice of any papal procedural orders against Bury St Edmunds which might reach him, for the pope would not 'knowingly' commit their causes to him.[38] The canonists were worried about papal mandates obtained by *subreptio* or *obreptio*, a problem that had also bedevilled the use of imperial rescripts in Rome; they worked out the theory that the reservation 'si preces veritate nitantur',[39] which occurred expressly in some, should be tacitly assumed in all papal rescripts.[40]

The English kings and their councillors also realized, of course, that writs based on one-sided complaints led to contradiction and injustice and to the very disorder which they were supposed to combat. They were torn between quick, authoritative orders (with the danger of injustice) and full judicial proceedings (which could be too meticulous and slow). They found themselves faced with the old choice between *jussio* and *jurisdictio*, and were learning that there was no short cut to justice. What was to be done? One solution was to stop interfering in legal matters through orders of redress altogether and leave everything to the existing law courts; but the pressure for royal intervention and the crisis of the law and the law courts were too great for that. The only other solution was to judicialize royal interventions, i.e. to surround them with the necessary judicial guarantees, to ensure fair examination of the merits of the case and the arguments and elements of proof involved, along procedural lines indicated in the royal writ. This stage was clearly reached under Stephen and in the early years of Henry II. It went a good deal further than the ambiguous *juste* or *recte* that had occasionally been added to various orders of restitution.[c] We find writs prescribing a fully fledged examination and a well specified means of judicial enquiry, as a condition for carrying out the royal order of redress, on the following lines: 'if by a sworn inquest in the county court of N. it appears that the claim of A against B is justified, then promptly give A full possession of the land in question'. Thus, for example, the writ of Stephen addressed to Walter fitz Gilbert and his reeve of Maldon, which says: 'if the canons of St. Martin's, London, can show that Osward of Maldon has "unjustly and without judgment" disseised them of their burgage land of Maldon, then I order that you cause them to be reseised'.[41]

Clearer still is the following writ of Stephen concerning the canons' marsh in Maldon, addressed to Richard de Lucy, local justice of London and Essex, and Maurice, sheriff of Essex: 'cause a recognition to be made through the oath of lawful men, who know the truth, of the hundreds of Maldon, Dengie and Thurstable to

[c] *Juste resaisias* could mean 'give seisin, but make sure that no injustice is involved', but also 'give seisin as you are ordered, thus restoring justice'. See a writ of Henry I for the abbey of Abingdon telling Hugh de Bocland, sheriff of Berkshire, to go to Abingdon and reseise the abbey of all the lands which Modbert, who administered the abbey from 1097 to 1100, had alienated and to make the church 'justly' have these lands, so that the king should hear no further complaints (*Chronicon de Abingdon*, ed. Stevenson, II, 86; *Regesta Regum Anglo-Normannorum*, II, nr 521, p. 8 A.D. 1100–1).

discover if the canons of St. Martin's, London, were seised of their marsh in Maldon until the day that Walter fitz Gilbert left for Jerusalem; if this is so recognized, then I order that they shall be reseised'.[42] Writs addressed to private parties, local justices or sheriffs (and their bailiffs), feudal lords who held courts or the reeves and burgesses of certain towns, following the pattern 'if plaintiff A can show (through some mode of proof specified or not) that he was unjustly disseised, then restore him in his possession', were frequent in the early years of Henry II.[43] But there was as yet nothing uniform or systematic about this. It was a gradual development and the old, purely executive writs had not disappeared. Also the judicial enquiry involved was left to local justices or sheriffs or feudal lords, and although recognitions were frequently indicated as the mode of proof this was not always so.

All this changed with Henry II's assizes: henceforth royal redress of injustice would be given through the king's (itinerant) justices and follow judicial procedures of which the jury was the keystone. What had been developing uncertainly and tentatively for years became a new body of law and a new judicial institution, the Common Law and the central courts. The course of events appears to have been as follows. In 1166 and following years Henry II engaged in a nation-wide offensive to maintain law and order by sending his justices throughout the country to try criminals brought before them by juries of indictment. Violence had increased as a consequence of civil strife under Stephen and Matilda and Henry II took sweeping measures directed from the centre, to be carried out not by the local courts, which he rightly considered inadequate, but by his own itinerant justices. We have seen the chronology of their eyres in the previous chapter. We know from the Assizes of Clarendon and Northampton how they were to deal with such crimes as murder, arson, theft, robbery and falsification. But we also know, from the entries in the pipe rolls parallel with these eyres, that the royal justices dealt at the same time with lesser offences such as unjust disseisins of land, which were a social plague: it has rightly been said that 'if thieving was the everyday vice of the labouring population, disseisin was the crime of the upper classes and a national scourge for centuries, until the land ceased to be the only foundation of power and standing'.[44] It is clear that a method of quickly,[d] forcefully and judicially restoring people to

[d] Novel disseisin permitted no essoins by defendants.

40

the peaceful possession of their land was a great advantage for public order (which Henry II strove to restore as it had been in the golden days of his grandfather). It was also a first-class way of gaining popularity among ordinary free men: in an age when almost everyone lived off the land, security in its possession was comparable to security of employment in our own industrial time.[45]

Thus the royal justices, touring the country like the Frankish *missi dominici*, were instructed to punish people who had recently (the prosecution of serious crime was also concerned with recent cases) and unjustly disseised somebody of his land (and were presented to them on that charge), and to reseise the lawful possessors. The justices were also told to establish whether any lawful heir had been refused seisin of the land to which he was entitled by the lord and if so, to put him in possession of his inheritance and to amerce the lord – another important step to ensure security of tenure. The assizes of Henry II were clearly in the nature of criminal investigations and prosecutions undertaken by a government mindful of public order,[46] but the mechanism used by the justices in eyre came also to be used to give redress on private plaint to parties whose claims were of a civil nature and for whom the criminal aspect (royal amercement) was incidental.

Thus out of an old tradition of royal intervention on private complaint and the penal initiatives of Henry II arose a set of actions to obtain redress from royal justices for a certain number of specified wrongs, falling within well established limitations. The judicialization of the old measures of redress was accomplished and the royal writs, which at first set out to avoid judicial proceedings, became documents initiating just that – but in the royal courts. Gradually more of these forms of action were evolved so that most of the disturbances of private rights could be dealt with by an appropriate action in the central courts. All this was royal, dealt with and enforced by central justices and officers and not by regional personnel. One by one the various aspects of landowning were protected by appropriate actions, beginning with appropriate writs.

To solve the question of where the greatest right in the land ultimately rested (which might entail obscure arrangements going back several generations), the parties could still go to the local court with a *breve de recto* and risk battle – a very dangerous and uncertain mode of proof where God was supposed to answer questions that human minds could not cope with. But why resort to this extreme step and undergo the solemn and cumbersome procedure on right, if there were other and better means of adequately protecting oneself on all matters concerning the practical advantages of right in land, i.e. peacefully possessing and exploiting it, receiving it from the lord on the death of one's ancestor, being able to present a new parson for one's church, to rebuke anyone trespassing on one's land, to establish that it was frankalmoin and not liable to secular services and so on? The process on right was never abolished, but what was the use of bothering with that obscure and academic question and risking death in judicial combat, if for all the practical advantages which that right entailed one could resort to the new and efficient actions applied in the royal courts?

Let us look at some of the early writs in detail. First the Common Law writs based on the four 'petty' assizes, i.e. the four enactments of Henry II other than the Grand Assize of Windsor. The most famous and important was the assize of 'novel disseisin', i.e. of recent dispossession. 'Assize' could refer to the jury whose verdict was the key-element in these proceedings. Alternatively it could be used for the whole action, which was begun by the plaintiff obtaining a writ of novel disseisin. 'Assize' could also refer to the royal enactment which set in motion the systematic prosecution of recent disseisins and eventually led to private plaintiffs being able to bring the action of novel disseisin. This royal enactment was probably made in 1166 (certainly not later), when the general eyre went out, charged with the enforcement of the famous Assize of Clarendon on serious crime.[47] Royal protection of seisin entered a new phase: no occasional orders to restore seisin to plaintiffs here and there, but a systematic, national campaign, directed from the centre. The first entries of amercements for 'disseisin against the assize' appear in the Pipe Roll of 1166[48] and continue for a few years, coinciding with the duration of the first wave of general eyres (A.D. 1166–70).[49] There is every reason to believe that this first drive against unjust disseisins was conceived as a temporary measure, just as the Assize of Clarendon and the general eyres connected with it: after 1170 the general eyres stop and so do the fines for unlawful disseisin. But in 1175 the general eyres were revived – in 1176 the Assize of Northampton was issued[50] – and the unlawful disseisins reappear in the pipe rolls: they are numerous for 1175, 1176 and particularly for 1177; they drop to almost nothing for

42

1178 which was a critical year for the general eyres, as we have seen. Thus the two periods of general eyres and the two first periods of amercements for unlawful disseisin mark exceptional royal drives against various forms of unlawful behaviour. Afterwards, with the justices in eyre established as a permanent feature, the flow of unlawful disseisins became a regular element in the pipe rolls throughout the reign, never surpassing the peak of 1177, but surpassing, right at the end of the reign, the peak of 1168. By this time however, the prosecution of unlawful disseisins was already a well established civil action at the disposal of all free landholders, against payment of a moderate fee for a writ of novel disseisin.[51]

The text of the assize, presumably issued in 1166, has not been conserved. This is the case with other English and Norman enactments of Henry II and need not unduly amaze us.[52] It is conceivable that the prosecution of unlawful disseisins was an afterthought, a task added, by word of mouth or by a separate writ to the justices,[e] to those mentioned in the Assize of Clarendon (as the justices were ready to start their eyres). It is, of course, also possible that a 'clerical error' is the explanation.[53] One thing is certain, in the Assize of Northampton there was an article dealing specially with the repression of recent unlawful disseisins and that text has come down to us.[54] The action permitted whoever had been unlawfully disseised of his free tenement to recover it on the basis of a verdict by a jury, within certain time limits before royal judges. The latter were also to amerce the disseisor, and give damages to the disseisee.[55]

What was the time limit within which the action had to be brought? In England – as opposed to Normandy – this was not a certain number of years or harvests, but some well known, fixed date. As we have no legislative text before 1176 we can only guess what the first date may have been: several considerations militate in favour of the coronation of Henry II in 1154.[56] In 1176, as we have seen, the time limit was fixed at the 'return of the king in

---

[e] The latter possibility is suggested by the expression 'disseisin *super breve regis*' in Pipe Roll 12 Henry II, pp. 7, 10. In 1170 Henry II held the Inquest of Sheriffs to fight disorders of a different kind, but also using juries of indictment and carried out by itinerant barons; it contained a chapter ordering 'inquiratur per omnes episcopatus quid et quantum et qua de causa archidiaconi vel decani *injuste et sine judicio* ceperint, et hoc totum scribatur' (*c.* 12) and, as a matter of conjecture, I feel that the order to prosecute recent disseisins in 1166(?) may have been drafted in a similar way (Stubbs, *Select Charters*, p. 177).

England after he made peace with his son', i.e. May 1175; in Glanvill the time limit was the latest crossing of the king to Normandy. These short time limits justified the name *de nova dissaisina*, first occurring in the Pipe Roll of 1181,[57] which triumphed over such names as 'the assize on disseisin' or 'the action of disseisin against the assize'. The assize and the action based on it offered protection of tenure, i.e. the peaceful possession and exploitation of free land, at a time when land was the essential form of wealth, the basis of almost everyone's livelihood and the great source of power and prestige. Leaving aside the intricate question of the greater right, or ownership as we might now say, it aimed at quickly undoing recent unwarranted disturbances of seisin, carried out 'unjustly and without judgment'.[58]

The classic action of novel disseisin, a fruit of Henry II's reign, was the culmination of a very long royal preoccupation with seisin, witnessed by numerous orders to restore possession, with or without certain forms of judicial enquiry. It was not the preoccupation with seisin that was new, but its systematic judicial form in the hands of the royal justices and the fact that it was now at the disposal of all free men. Seisin and the protection of seisin – as opposed to right and the lawsuits connected with it – were very old notions, with roots in Germanic *gewere*, feudal *vestitura* and ecclesiastical ideas on *spoliatus ante omnia restituendus* and *nemo placitet dissaisitus* of the early Middle Ages.[59] It was not the renaissance of Roman Law in Bologna which revealed this: people had known for centuries that seisin and right – *possessio* and *proprietas* being the corresponding Roman notions – were two different things and that measures concerning seisin could be followed by litigation on right, but could just as well be taken for their own sake and without further litigation. So it had been in the past and so it remained after novel disseisin had taken shape.[60] There is no need to see influence of the *Corpus Juris Civilis* here,[61] let alone of the canonistic *actio spolii*, which is of a later date,[62] nor was novel disseisin conceived as a preliminary to a process on right.

Of course, people who lost their case on seisin could try an action on right,[63] but this was an exceedingly rare phenomenon and the reason is not far to seek. Seisin was not merely a question of material but of lawful detention: 'seisin must include some modicum of right, and it is hardly possible to say where seisin ends and right begins'.[64] The question put to the jury was not only whether A had

44

been disseised without judgment, but whether he had been disseised *unjustly* and without judgment: the jury had to go into the legal situation and if a jury of twelve lawful freemen had found that a man had not been disseised unjustly the chances that a subsequent jury of twelve knights in a process on right would find that he had, after all, the greater right were very small. It is not because a negative judgment on seisin leaves the loser the theoretical liberty to start a plea on right that his real chances are good.[65]

Some historians, who admire the legal achievements of the Anglo-Saxon and the genius of the Angevin kings, cannot say a good word for the Normans, who constitute a sort of *medium aevum* between two glorious epochs. In their view the barbaric Normans brought utter darkness, which was relieved only by the light of Henry II's reign, when 'genius was at work' and the great 'Angevin leap forward' took place. In this perspective the period from William the Conqueror to Stephen is covered with the mantle of Noah and the action of novel disseisin had no history and certainly no Norman roots, but was suddenly revealed after a few nights of deep thinking.[f]

But the documents tell a different story, of the protection of seisin by Norman kings, and its increasingly judicial character (documented by several writs), followed by the repression of unlawful disseisins in Henry II's eyres as part of his fight against lawlessness (documented by the pipe rolls), and finally the emergence in the second half of his reign of novel disseisin as a judicial remedy of a civil nature, the most striking of the actions composing the nascent Common Law (documented by the pipe rolls, Glanvill, the early surviving returned writs – the oldest going back to A.D. 1199 and one or two even to the earlier years of Richard I[66] – and the earliest assize rolls). What remains obscure in this story is how the wording of the writ of novel disseisin – as opposed to the process – developed. There is no reason to believe that the wording, as we find it in Glanvill and the earliest surviving writs, was fixed right at the beginning: too much change and experiment went on throughout the reign. Also the classic writ of novel disseisin was a pure writ of summons to appear in court, and was entirely judicial, i.e. it

---

f Sir F. Pollock (see p. 99) thought the Common Law so majestic that it must have been of divine origin, but he failed to convert me and I can steer clear of such theological explanations of the rise of the Common Law.

45

belonged to the final stage, when the development from executive to judicial instrument had reached its logical conclusion.[67]

I consider it highly probable that the writ went – say in the 1160s and 1170s – through a stage where it retained an executive element, in the familiar form (which we shall meet in the writ *praecipe*) 'give back seisin to the plaintiff or else appear before my justices'. I cannot produce an actual example, at least from England, to prove this,[68] but fortunately Henry II's assizes operated in Normandy as well, along corresponding lines, with similar writs for similar incidents, and among them we find the writ of novel disseisin. The interesting point about this Norman specimen is – and it was Professor Yver who was able to draw attention to it – that it follows the 'give back seisin, or else plead before my justices' pattern, belonging, no doubt, to an intermediate stage between the archaic order to restore seisin and the formal writ of summons of Glanvill, which was never reached in Normandy.[69] This strengthens my opinion that the wording in Glanvill was recent; its opening phrase 'conquestus est mihi' was possibly suggested to the clerks of the chancery by papal examples.[70] However this may be, the wording of the writ is less important than the rise and development of the action and it is not because of a difference in phraseology that one should deny continuity between the earliest interventions on seisin and the later Common Law actions. Also one should be allowed to trace the early antecedents of the Common Law writs without incurring the reproach of anachronism[71] – after all, that is what Bigelow attempted to do in a pioneering effort that did not receive sufficient recognition.[72]

The writ of novel disseisin was returnable, i.e. contained the clause, addressed to the sheriff, who had much preparatory work to do, 'and have there (before me or my justices on such a date) the summons and this writ (with the names of the jurors endorsed on it) and the names of the sureties'. The returning of writs was a practical device of control, but did not affect the basic conception of novel disseisin as a quick but judicial remedy for recent unlawful loss of seisin, in the royal court and on the basis of a jury verdict: too great an importance should not be attached to it. Nor was it in any way astonishing or illogical that these originating writs, issued by one royal office, the chancery, should 'return' to another, the central courts. It was, after all, an established practice that the writ on which one pleaded was put before the court. The writ of right was put by the beneficiary before the local court mentioned in it and was read at the outset;[73] in the same way returnable writs were put – by the sheriff who was given various judicial tasks which used to be left to litigants – before the justices to whom they gave authority. It is normal to assume that the writ in the 60s and 70s mentioned all the essentials: the parties and the land, an order for the summons of parties and jurors and a date for the hearing before the justices; at what moment the clause about returning the writ with mention of various elements of procedural importance, was added is one of the many uncertainties surrounding the evolution of the wording of the writ – it certainly appears in the Norman, more 'primitive' writ of novel disseisin.

The second of the petty assizes is that of mort d'ancestor. The action dealt with inheritance, more precisely with the formal act by which the lord of the land gave seisin to the heir of his deceased tenant. This ceremony had to be performed, for the heir could not automatically keep his inheritance, but no lord could withhold it from a lawful heir. It was as a weapon against an unwarranted refusal by the lord to give due seisin that the action was devised. At a later stage it could also be brought against another tenant (except a kinsman). The pattern is strikingly similar to that of novel disseisin. The action dealt with seisin – not the ultimate question of right, that could take the courts generations back and entail endless discussions and enquiries;[74] it took place before royal justices, was confined within certain time limits[75] and the verdict of a jury of freemen was decisive; it was also launched as part of a great inquest by justices in eyre and developed into a civil action at the disposal of private plaintiffs. The questions put to the jury were the following: 'was the ancestor of the plaintiff seised as of fee (i.e. hereditarily) and in his demesne (i.e. directly exploited by him and not handed to another tenant or vassal) of the land M. on the day of his death;[g] is the plaintiff the nearest heir?' Although royal interventions in favour of individuals who could not enter their inheritance had been known for generations, art. 4 of the Assize of Northampton definitely established the action. The assize, after explaining that seisin should not be withheld from heirs, ordered the following: 'if the lord of a fee refuses to give seisin to the heirs of the deceased man which they demand, the justices of the lord king shall cause a recognition to be made thereof by twelve lawful men, to find out what seisin the

[g] Not a new question for English juries, see Domesday Book, I, fol. 375v.

47

dead man had when he died and according to their recognition seisin will be restored to the heir, and who acts against this and is
attainted thereof shall be in the king's mercy'.[76] Payments by heirs
to bring the action – 'pro recognitione de morte patris sui' and the
like – occur in the pipe rolls from 1179 onwards. The early assize
rolls also betray its great popularity. Together, novel disseisin and
mort d'ancestor ensured peaceful possession for the ordinary freeman and his heirs. Glanvill gives the text of the writ by which the
action was brought. About possible older formulations we are as
badly informed as with novel disseisin.[77]

The third in this series, the assize *utrum*, is less important. It
really started as a preliminary suit to decide 'whether' (*utrum*) a
certain fee was lay or ecclesiastical; according to the answer, the
case belonged to the lay or the Church courts (a touchy and often
difficult point in the twelfth century). But more was involved than
the legal nature of a tenure and the competence of a court, for the
spiritual services due for an ecclesiastical tenure (frankalmoin,
franca elemosina) were very different from the more material ones
that weighed on a knight's fee. Since those services were often the
very cause of the dispute, the decision on the nature of the tenement decided the real issue. Consequently, in course of time, *utrum*
became an action in its own right, asked and paid for by private
parties,[78] protecting the interests of parsons, i.e. the free alms of
their churches. Eventually it took its place beside the other actions
concerning various aspects of land law, which appeared before royal
justices and were decided by the verdict of a jury. Even before
Henry II the question whether a tenure was lay or not had occasionally been answered by a recognition on royal command.[79] In
the Constitutions of Clarendon, where the king put on record a
number of principles concerning royal and ecclesiastical courts, c. 9
laid down that in a dispute concerning a tenure which the cleric
considered as frankalmoin and the layman as a lay fee, this question
was to be decided by a jury of twelve lawful men before the chief
justiciar, and according to the outcome the plea was to go to an
ecclesiastical or the royal court.[80] Quite soon recognitions would
take place before the justices in eyre, like the other petty assizes
and originate with a comparable writ[81] and would be so final that it
was appropriately called the 'parson's writ of right'. As it came to
be reserved exclusively for parsons for claims on the land belonging
to their churches, it had a narrow scope and was not frequently used.

The fourth of the petty assizes was called 'darrein presentment' or 'last presentation'. It dealt with the right of landowners to present clerics to the bishop for appointment in their proprietary churches. The right of patronage in England and Normandy was known 'by some *bizarrerie*'[82] as 'advowson' and we find the terms *advocatus* and *advocatia*, where we would expect the common European usage of *patronus* and *patronatus*. It is not clear why this is so, but advowson, a relic of pre-Gregorian times, was certainly a source of income and prestige – presentation was only one of its elements – and Henry II decided to protect it, like other elements of landowning. He did so by a device that followed closely the pattern of the other assizes, i.e. a recognition before royal justices to settle the urgent question of who was to present – against payment of a lump sum or promise of a rent – a new parson to a vacant church, leaving open the possibility of enquiring who had ultimately the best title to the advowson (for which a writ of right could be brought). In 1179 the Third Lateran Council gave the presentation to the bishop, if the benefice was not filled within three months.[83] As traditional litigation on the right of advowson would probably last a good deal longer than three months, this meant a potential loss for the landowners and a gain for the bishops. It is very probable that this consideration[h] led Henry II to introduce an assize concerning advowsons of churches – mentioned first in 1180 – on the familiar pattern, resembling most closely that of mort d'ancestor and dealing only with the following essential question (and therefore suitably quick): 'which patron presented in time of peace[84] the last parson, whose death left the church vacant?'[85] Leaving aside the question of ultimate right (with what right had the previous parson been presented?), the justices directed that whoever presented the previous time was considered in seisin of the advowson and could therefore present again; his candidate was appointed for life, whatever the result of a possible later plea on right of the advowson. Juries and justices did their job so well that the action led normally to a final settlement of

[h] Not any desire on his part to channel pleas on presentation to his court, since he had expressly claimed litigation on advowson for his court in c. 1 of the Constitutions of Clarendon (Stubbs, *Select Charters*, p. 164). During the reign of Stephen and the early years of Henry II disputes over advowson normally went to courts Christian, Henry II then made and maintained his claim in spite of a flat rejection by Alexander III; see Cheney, *From Becket to Langton*, pp. 7, 109–10.

disputes on advowson, leaving the old plea on right of advowson to decay.[86]

The writs of the petty assizes brought a considerable flow of cases before the royal justices, but had to share that honour with a rival, whose historical interest is as great as its legal importance, *Praecipe*. This writ has other titles to fame than its fleeting appearance in cl. 34 of Magna Carta to which I shall turn in a moment.[87] It is for example the first writ in Glanvill (I, 6). The petty assizes concerned only a limited category of complaints: unlawful disseisin, unlawful refusal to give seisin to an heir, disputes about the presentation of a new parson and about parsons' rights. This was far from exhausting the gamut of contention and litigation and left undecided the question of 'the greater right', which some litigants might want to see settled by the courts: the assizes operated within strict limits. Cases that fell outside their scope could, of course, be brought before the local courts along traditional lines of procedure. They might also be brought before the royal courts if the crown was willing to receive them there. It is for those cases that the writ *praecipe* was used.[1] For all practical purposes this writ was a writ of summons – addressed to the defendant through the sheriff – to answer in the king's court about dower withheld, a debt unpaid, a claim to advowson, ownership of land and the like, and yet this writ of summons, which Glanvill simply calls a *breve de summonitione*, began with an order to the defendant to restore the land or to pay the debt to the plaintiff: unless he did, he was to plead on the claim in the king's court.[88] It seems odd, at first sight, to summon somebody to appear in court and to begin by telling him to do what the plaintiff demands – one would rather expect such an order after trial and judgment; nor is it normal for a commission to a court to try a case, to open with an order of restitution. The reason for this anomaly lies in the history of *praecipe*. It was not devised *ex nihilo* as a writ of summons for the royal courts, but started as an executive order of redress addressed to an alleged wrongdoer. In the course of time this sort of order was judicialized in that the alleged wrongdoer was given the chance to come and state his case in the king's court. The peculiar pattern of the writ *praecipe* reflects that stage: it was not redrafted after it had become a simple writ of summons, but

---

[1] For tenants in chief the king's court was normal, but many others succeeded in bringing their cases there.

nobody expected the opening command – a mere fossil – to be carried out.

The history of *praecipe* begins with the numerous peremptory orders to do or stop doing something, sent by the Norman kings to various people after hearing the complaints of their opponents. These writs could concern ownership of a whole manor (see further), or a portion of fish,[89] the duty of recalcitrant tenants to do service to their lord or the right of the monks of Christ Church Canterbury to toll their bells before those of St Augustine's[90] – and, of course, the restoration of seisin. Here are a few examples of this highly paternalistic technique of doing justice. A writ of Henry I peremptorily ordered archdeacon Almod to restore the manor of Sawbridge to the abbey of Thorney as well stocked as he had received it (possibly by way of lease or on the king's behalf during a vacancy in the abbacy).[91] In the early years of this reign abbot Faritius of Abingdon had acquired the mill of Langford near Oxford from William of Seacourt, son of Anskill, but after the abbot's death in 1117, William, who had even received money for the mill, went to the king and complained that he had alienated his mill under pressure (of debt?) and not of his free will. Thereupon the king ordered that the mill be restored to him.[92] A third example comes from the reign of Stephen, who wrote in 1136 or 1138 to Rainald de Muschamp and his sister Cecily, commanding them to return to the monks of Durham the land of Heatherslaw which their brother Thomas, whose heirs they were, had offered upon the altar when he became a monk.[93] These orders were often accompanied by threats that some royal justice or sheriff would see to their execution if the addressee was disobedient, and we have records of acts of restitution on royal command.[94]

There is no need to insist again on the disadvantages of this sort of executive justice, based on one-sided complaints and one-sided evidence. Writs of restitution led to visits from frantic opponents who swayed the king to undo what he had just done. In the case of the mill of Langford, for example, we are told that a delegation of monks led by Walter, the chaplain of William de Bockland, soon persuaded the king, 'recognizing the truth', to order that the mill should change hands once more – a final act of restitution which William accepted and confirmed by placing a symbolic rod on the altar.[95] We hear too much of restitutions ordered 'since abbot so and so says that you have no right in that land',[96] nor are stipulations lacking that a certain writ was to be executed even if writs to the contrary effect were produced.[97] Unjust measures and farcical situations were the fatal results of these high-handed attempts to keep order in that violent society and there is no need to explain the circumstances which had caused them. The remedy, as we have seen, was to surround these royal interventions with a guarantee that would allow for serious judicial enquiry without giving up the real advantages of royal intervention. Several possibilities existed and experiments were carried out, notably the interrogation of a local jury, but the one that won the day was giving the opponent the opportunity to state his case and show that the beneficiary of the writ had made an unjustified complaint. The pattern is simple: ' I order you to restore the land unless you will plead to show why you should not.' Although the possibility of pleading in a local court was sometimes offered,[98] the most normal course was for litigation in the king's court: it was logical that the king himself should see what arguments were brought forward against his orders and judge for himself.

The following writs of Henry I and Stephen clearly follow such a pattern. In a writ of 1112–21 to Stephen of Aumale, confirmation is given of Hornsea Mere to the abbot of St Mary's York and prohibition is notified specifically for Geoffrey de Spineto to fish there but, the royal writ adds, 'if anyone makes any claim concerning this, let him come and plead before me'.[99] Another writ of Henry I, of 1101–6, puts it the other way round, by telling Nicholas, the sheriff of Staffordshire, to appear before the *curia regis* on the first day of Lent if he wants to deraign the land of Coton-in-the-Elms against the abbot of Burton; otherwise, if he does not want to appear in court, he is to let the abbot have the land undisturbed.[100] In a writ according to the more usual scheme, Stephen, in 1150–4, ordered earl William of Warenne to leave the land of the monks of Reading in Catshill in peace and to give back whatever he had taken away there, but if he had any claim, he was to come in the king's court and full right would be done to him.[101] The pattern 'render the land in N. to A. or else come and plead in my court' had clearly developed, before: under Henry II, it became a widely used stereotype of Common Law. In the course of his reign the initial order became a meaningless form, an irrelevant relic of the past.[j] We do not

---

[j] But a relic with financial consequences, for the Common Law imposed an amercement on the defendant who lost this civil action, for the good

know when this happened, and it is the sort of gradual process upon which a date can seldom be put – who knows, for example, when exactly final concords ceased to be agreements in real lawsuits and became mere documents of conveyance, the litigation involved being purely fictitious? But we can suppose that the success of the justices in eyre and of the petty assizes in the 1160s and 1170s, together with the general tendency towards judicialization played a rôle. Probably about the same time certain technical improvements were introduced, mirrored in the formulation of the Common Law writ as we know it, i.e. the summoning of the defendant by the sheriff, to whom the writ was addressed, instead of by the plaintiffs (who must have been greatly relieved that this hazardous task was taken off their shoulders) and the obligation of the sheriff to appear at the hearing before the royal justices with the writ (and the summoners). The return of the writ was a practical device completely in line with the increasing bureaucratization of the time and its careful keeping of records; it put the commission to hear the case before the judges and immediately showed them the essential data of the case.

In Glanvill we find nine writs *praecipe*,[102] to which very soon covenant, account and the very important writs of entry were added. The great innovation in the latter was that instead of stating vaguely that the plaintiff was 'deforced' of his land or debt, they specified the precise circumstances under which the alleged wrong had been caused. Thus, for example, the writ of entry *sur disseisin* could be used by A against B who had obtained 'entry' on his land through C, who had unjustly and without judgment disseised A;[103] one can see here how this (and other) writs of entry supplemented the older

reason that he had disobeyed the king's initial order. See Coke on Littleton, 126*b*, a quotation from Coke's own report on Vaughan's case, 39 & 40 Eliz., 5 Rep. 49*a* (*anno* 1597), with reference to the Year Book of 22 Edward III, fol. 1 and A. Fitzherbert, *La Graunde Abridgement* (London, 1577), *v*° Amercement, 16 (fol. 36*v*) and 26 (fols. 36*v*–37*r*); see also Beecher's case, 8 Rep. 61 *b* (*anno* 1609). I am greatly obliged to Dr J. Barton, of Merton College, Oxford, who drew my attention to this point and very kindly provided the references. T. F. T. Plucknett briefly indicated the executive origin of the writ process when he wrote: 'The common law is the product of administrative processes, evolved in the curia regis ... The common law crystallized around procedures ... These administrative activities increased until it was finally realized that they were truly legal in their nature, supplanting older legal processes.' 'The Relations between Roman Law and English Common Law down to the sixteenth century', *Univ. Toronto Law Journal*, 3 (1939–40), 32.

action of novel disseisin, which lay only against the disseisor himself. Although the writs of entry *eo nomine* do not occur until after Glanvill, the first steps in their direction are clearly present in his Treatise. Take for example the writ *ad terminum qui praeteriit*, known as writ of gage (x, 9). The writ concerns the very specific case of a creditor who after being paid (or offered payment) refuses to restore the land, which he held in gage 'for a length of time that is passed'.[104] The writs of entry, the widest class in the form *praecipe*, vastly expanded the scope of the Common Law courts and, together with trespass, made possible 'a remedy for every wrong': 'if some new wrong were perpetrated, then a new writ might be invented to meet it'.[105]

I referred above to *Praecipe* and Magna Carta. An illuminating note by M. T. Clanchy makes the following development plausible. There is no doubt that the *praecipe quod reddat* for land (Glanvill, I, 6) drew litigation into the king's court that did not belong there and caused 'a free man to lose his court'. There was, however, no such danger if the land was held directly from the Crown or if the lord of the land did not mind the case going to the king's court. The application of Magna Carta, cl. 34, meant that a proprietary action for land could henceforth be initiated in the king's court only for land held *in capite* or if the lord of the land agreed to let the case go to the king's court. For the Common Law writs, clause 34, which accorded perfectly with feudal law, led to the disappearance of the writ *praecipe* of Glanvill, I, 6 and its replacement by the writ *praecipe in capite* for land held directly from the king,[106] and by the writ *praecipe quia dominus remisit curiam suam*, for land held from a feudal lord, who had passed the case over to the royal court.[107] These two new writs are simply the old *praecipe* of Glanvill, I, 6, to which the appropriate formulas demanded by the new situation were added. All this applies only to the *praecipe* of Glanvill, I, 6, the proprietary action on land, since the other writs of *praecipe*, i.e. for debt, covenant, account and detinue and, of course, the popular writs of entry (opening with *praecipe* but containing the formula *in quas non habet ingressum nisi*) continued to be used, unaffected by clause 34 of the Great Charter.[108]

I shall say no more about these thirteenth-century writs and I shall be content to refer you to Mr Hall's learned and comprehensive commentary on the Registers of Writs, which he has so admirably edited with Miss De Haas. But I have mentioned 'trespass' and I cannot help drawing attention very briefly to it, not only because with *praecipe* and the petty assizes it was one of the three great classes of returnable writs that originated pleading in the royal courts, but also because its form of a summons *ostensurus quare* was the logical conclusion of the development of *praecipe*. In the form *ostensurus quare*, of which the trespass writs are the most important examples, we have a writ summoning a defendant in the royal court 'to show why' he has done a certain wrong or omitted some rightful action – exactly as in *praecipe* – but without the initial purely fictitious order that characterized *praecipe*: form and function coincided at last. With *ostensurus quare* the development from the purely executive order of redress to the purely judicial writ of summons was formally concluded.

Judicialization was not an iron law, from which no executive writ could escape. The writ of 'naifty', an ancient word for serfdom, is a case in point; its Latin name was *de nativis*, literally 'natives', i.e. those 'born' into servile status, who were also known as 'Anglici', because the mass of the peasant population was of English, and not Norman descent. Being a great landowner was not much use if one's serfs ran away, and some of the earliest royal writs ordered categorically that certain serfs who had run away from their masters should be arrested and brought back to the manor where they belonged. This writ *de nativis* followed the ordinary police pattern: 'I order that Eudo my steward be seized of the manor of Dereman and all the men who left after the latter's death are to return, with their chattels.'[109] Or: 'The king to the sheriff, greeting. See to it that the fugitive villeins of such an abbey are brought back with their chattels, and more particularly their serf who is now on the land of such a lord';[110] or 'The king to the local justiciar and sheriff of Essex, greeting. I order that the bishop of Winchester shall have his fugitive serf Ulwin Mud and his chattels as they were deraigned.'[111] Numerous writs from the early years of Henry II order his justices, sheriffs and bailiffs to restore to various landowners all their 'nativi et fugitivi cum catallis suis' who had fled since the death of Henry I (in other words since the beginning of the unmentionable reign of Stephen).[112] It was very useful as royal orders did not stop at internal administrative frontiers or suffer from the lack of competence of sheriffs or local courts to act outside their geographical boundaries – and one can imagine that a runaway villein would put a large distance between himself (and possibly his new master), and the glebe to which he was (or should have been) attached. These primitive orders for the arrest and return of villeins were bound to run into the familiar trouble: what happened if the victim claimed not to be a serf at all, or if he or his new master claimed that he had changed masters in a regular way? One can imagine the little war of writs, with protestations leading to a new writ countermanding the first.

As a result, we may feel, the writ ought in course of time to have been judicialized into a writ initiating pleading on status between the alleged villein and his master or between masters claiming the same villein. But for some obscure reason this did not happen – possibly because the villeins as a class could not put up the same resistance to royal orders as the landowners or because the capture of villeins was too urgent or it was found too difficult to comprehend the contradictory claims of masters and the fugitive's claim to freedom all in one originating writ. When the great wave of judicialization was over, the writ of naifty emerged unaffected, in the shape of a peremptory order to the sheriff 'justly and without delay to cause R. to have M. his villein and fugitive, with all his chattels and his whole household, wherever he shall be found in your jurisdiction (unless it be in the king's demesne), who fled from his land since the king's coronation; anyone who detains him unjustly will do so on pain of forfeiture'.[113] But what happened if M. – maybe a namesake of poor Ulwin Mud whom we have just met – objected to the execution of the writ on the ground that he was a free man?[114] The answer is that M. could complain to the king that someone was trying to reduce him to villein status and obtain a writ *de libertate probanda*, which would start litigation on his status before the royal justices.[115] In other words, we have here the old war of writ and counter-writ as an established procedure of the Common Law.

Royal will and coercion were the historic mainsprings of Common Law actions and accounted for the unmistakable police flavour of its civil actions in later times: it was not only in criminal actions that it rained amercements wherever the king's justices sat. People were continually ordered to come and show why they had done or not done one thing or another, and were continually being amerced for an immense variety of offences. Some were amerced for trying to stay away from the Common Law courts (and from serving on its juries), others for trying to gain access there (and obtain writs reserved for free men), and defendants even for losing a civil action

56

on a writ *praecipe*.[116] If, in Maitland's words, people could expect to be amerced at least once a year,[117] as we can expect at least one bad cold each winter, these eternal amercements must have been a great nuisance, even if they became less ruinous in course of time and had to leave a man's social position intact, to fit the 'measure of the delict' and to be assessed by a verdict of a jury.[118] That people put up with it all need not unduly surprise us, if we remember that the Norman regime was rooted in military conquest and occupation.

The complex system of courts, actions and recognitions forming the basis of the Common Law under Henry II was not peculiar to the English part of his domains, but operated with equal vigour in the Duchy of Normandy. There was a basic similarity on both sides of the Channel, as could be expected in two countries living in a state of great political and institutional symbiosis, under a common ruler and ruling class. There were, of course, differences in timing, terminology and various secondary aspects of the writ procedure, as might be predicted of two countries which conserved their own political existence. England and Normandy did not become one state, Normandy remained a duchy, never became part of the Kingdom of England, and conserved a strong sense of regional patriotism and pride. If, therefore, the study of the writ system within the boundaries of the Kingdom of England is justified, it is nevertheless rewarding to see what information can be gained from the parallel Norman development. I have quoted one example already, concerning the wording of the writ of novel disseisin, where the Norman story gave us a useful hint. Let us see what more we can learn from the events on the Lower Seine. The task is not at all difficult, thanks to the researches of such historians as Brunner, Haskins, Besnier and Yver. The basic fact is this: under Henry II a new system was established in Normandy. It was based on originating writs, recognitions and central courts, was similar to that in England and began at roughly the same time. It was described in law-books of great value at an early date, just as in England: the first part of the *Très Ancien Coutumier* is about fifteen years later than Glanvill. Let us have a closer look at some of the Norman writs, which were much less numerous and diversified than those in Glanvill. The writ of novel disseisin, known as the *requenoissant* (or recognition) *de nouvelle dissaisine,* applied within a shorter time limit, the last or last but one harvest. In other words as long as a plaintiff had not missed two harvests, he could bring the action: harvesting was the clearest sign of seisin.

It is impossible to tell exactly when the Norman action appeared and whether it was older or younger than its English counterpart;[119] it was certainly established before 1180, when traces of it are numerous in the Exchequer Roll. The wording of the writ, as we find it in the second part (c. 1220) of the *Très Ancien Coutumier* (LXXIII, 2), was in the archaic *praecipe* form and in the *Summa de Legibus* it was the only writ left with the archaic *praecipe* formula (XCIII, 1). The writ of mort d'ancestor had its equivalent in the *bref de saisine d'ancesseur*, but there were some interesting divergences. There is clear evidence in Normandy of the existence of two actions to gain possession of one's inheritance; one (possibly older) was at the disposal of the minor who claimed the land of his father (the action *de saisina patris*, or *de saisina orphani patris*),[120] the other (possibly more recent) could be used by others than minors and for the land of other ancestors than the father (the *bref de saisine d'ancesseur*). Both had in the *Très Ancien Coutumier* the form *praecipe* (LXXIV, 2, 3) and – another difference from the English writ – the question of the quality of 'nearest heir' was left, if it was posed, to a separate incidental inquest; also the time limit was short, being the last August. In the *Summa de Legibus Normannie* (XCVIII, 1) of the middle of the thirteenth century the wording has become that of a writ of summons (without *praecipe*) and the time limit has disappeared. The action is treated in terms similar to novel disseisin.

Little is known about the action *de presentatione ad ecclesiam*: this Norman writ appears as a purely judicial writ of summons in the *Très Ancien Coutumier* (LXXVII, 2). We find litigation on the presentation to a church in Cotentin in the court of the duke before a jury as early as 1159[121] and another case, concerning the church of Sap, older than 1164, involved a question of *praesentatio ecclesiae* and of *utrum pertinet ad feodum laicum*. The pure action *utrum*, or *de feodo et elemosina*, as it was called in Normandy, appeared with its completely judicial standard formulation in the *Très Ancien Coutumier* (LXXXVII, 1, 2) and in the *Summa de Legibus* (CXV, 1) and was at the disposal of laymen against clerics as well as vice versa. The writ of naifty was unknown in Normandy, and so was the *praecipe quod reddat* of Glanvill, I, 6. There were writs which brought litigation into the ducal courts, but they were purely judicial writs of summons. Such was the writ *de difforciante*

58

hereditatem (*T.A.C.*, LXXXV, 4), also known as *bref d'établie*, which corresponded to the writ in Glanvill, II, 15 as it allowed the defendant in an action on right to choose recognition in the ducal court instead of judicial combat. Such also were the writs *de feodo et vadio* (*T.A.C.*, LXXXVI, 1) and *de dote negata* (*Summa*, CI, 12) and some others. The rule *nemo tenetur respondere sine brevi regis* was unknown for the simple reason that no writ of right like the one in Glanvill, XII, 3 existed in Norman Law: the writ *rectum faciendi in curia ducis* (*T.A.C.*, XXX) was quite different as it ordered a lord who had refused to do right to his vassal, to see right done in the duke's court. The very complex system of Norman writ pleading, which I only touch upon here, gradually gave way in the later thirteenth century to French legal ideas and forms of process, based on Roman Law and Romano-canonical procedure.[122] Remarkably enough, the Anglo-Norman writ was spreading into Scotland from England while it was gradually eroded in Normandy. When, however, Scotland turned her back on the English legal system in the fourteenth century and moved slowly towards continental law, the Anglo-Norman system survived in England alone, turning the kingdom into a legal island in the western world.

It is well known that judicial centralization was not the exclusive privilege of England and Normandy: the century that produced Alexander III and Innocent III saw the rise of the papal *curia* as the centre of ecclesiastical law and law courts and the consequent 'papal descent into a vast ocean of litigation'.[123] I shall not enter into this complex subject at the end of a long chapter, but the rôle of papal rescripts shows so many similarities with royal writs that I feel compelled to mention them here, the more so since we can consult (in excerpt) the pioneering dissertation which Dr La Due has consecrated to this comparison.[124] In the course of the twelfth century the popes frequently intervened in disputes in favour of petitioners who had little hope with their local authorities. From the 1140s onwards in particular, increasing numbers of complaints were brought before them in appeal or in first instance and were made the object of papal rescripts. Some of these committed the complaints to papal judges delegate for investigation and adjudication in their country of origin, other cases were decided in Rome, often on the basis of the version and the material proffered by the plaintiffs only; papal orders to set things right then went out to their opponents, who were liable to take the road to Rome at once to obtain, with arguments and gifts, a countermanding order. We have already met this sort of muddle;[125] in Rome, the granting of papal rescripts on the basis of one-sided information eventually led to the rise of judicial office, charged with hearing both parties and studying their arguments before the rescripts were delivered. I mean, of course, the *audientia litterarum contradictarum*, which took shape in the papal Chancery under Innocent III and was presided over by the *auditor litterarum contradictarum*, who was at the same time an official of the Chancery and a judge of the curia. Here the rescripts were read in the presence of the parties or their procurators and objections of law or fact were made; the oldest surviving formularies with papal rescripts of this office go back to the 1220s and 1230s, roughly the time of the first Registers of Writs.[126] All this sounds very familiar to the student of Anglo-Norman writs, but the use of papal rescripts never developed into a legal system based on forms of action. They did not become the stereotyped initial documents of a limited number of actions, as even the delegation rescripts did not delineate the form and steps which the action was to take. There are several reasons for this. First, Romano-canonical procedure, followed by ecclesiastical courts from the twelfth century onwards, developed on quite different lines, not those of the old Roman formulary process or the Anglo-Norman forms of action, but of a procedural science with general concepts and rules for all classes of cases and all parts of substantive law. Secondly, the popes claimed the *plenitudo potestatis,* whereas the kings of England, who had issued no *Dictatus regis* comparable to the *Dictatus papae,* had to respect the rights of the local courts and extended their direct jurisdiction only in a limited number of specified complaints; strictly speaking the assizes left the question of right to the traditional courts and the writ *praecipe* could not be used to deprive a lord of his court. Bringing all ecclesiastical litigation encompassed by certain actions before the papal court was a practical impossibility for reasons of size. In the thirteenth century, by introducing the officialities and developing the appeal procedure a network of centrally controlled and streamlined courts was constructed, applying papal law and following Romano-canonical procedure. It removed much of the importance of the twelfth-century judges delegate.

In the meantime the English writ process was going from strength to strength on the basis laid in Henry Plantagenet's day. Indeed, as Lady Stenton says, 'it was Henry II with his returnable writs and his carefully built up bench of judges, through his own versatility and that of his great Justiciar, Rannulf de Glanville, who had started the wheel in perpetual motion which generated the English Common law'.[127] The success of the system was remarkable, the enthusiasm of the plaintiffs evident. It resulted from the quality of the professional royal justices: compare the intellectual level and technical standard (only slightly influenced by the revival of Roman Law) of Glanvill's Treatise with some of the helpless compilations of the earlier years of the century; it was also due to the coherence of the system, clearly understood as such in Glanvill, encompassing all free men in the same royal solicitude, and to the combination of royal efficiency with judicial guarantees. There is no doubt that this nascent Common Law owed much of its popularity to the mode of proof that was the heart of its procedure, the jury verdict. But this leads us to the history of evidence, which is reserved for the next chapter.

3

The jury in the royal courts

'Praecipio ut recognosci facias'

Ordeals, compurgation and juries were the essence of the law of evidence in the twelfth century. Some readers, who have leafed through old Treatises on Evidence – by W. Nelson or Sir Geoffrey Gilbert, or nearer to us, by S. M. Phillips, Sir James Stephen or J. Thayer[1] – may imagine that a chapter on evidence must be so full of technicalities as to frighten even the hardiest student away from 'the barren fields of law books'. This is not necessarily so. On the contrary, in the history of evidence the interaction of general culture and legal ideas can be followed most clearly. It is a field that belongs to psychological as well as legal history. It demonstrates the true position of the law in the general context of civilization: not as a marginal, abstruse technique of interest to specialists only, but part and parcel of the culture of any given period and one of its most important elements. The history of modes of proof does, of course, throw light on legal thinking and judicial organization, but it also illuminates the mentality, the attitude towards the supernatural and other aspects of the psychology of ordinary people – a very precious source indeed for those remote centuries where information is hard to come by. We know of many civilizations which have moved from ordeals to rational modes of proof, but I know of none where the transformation is as well documented as in Europe in the twelfth and thirteenth centuries. The relative profusion of source material matches the importance of the subject. The question of proof is evidently crucial, always and everywhere, for without adequate proof the best case may be lost; unfortunately it often baffles the mind, for so imperfect is intelligence, so frail human memory and so inarticulate or contradictory many witnesses that even with the best technical and scientific help the courts can be at a loss or make terrible mistakes.

Evidence is of exceptional importance because the Common Law took shape and developed round a specific mode of proof, the jury, and owed much of its stormy expansion to the advantages which the latter offered to the public. In the formative years of the twelfth century the fateful decision was taken and local juries of knights or ordinary freemen giving their verdict before royal justices became central in criminal and civil law, and remained there for many centuries – in criminal matters, till our own day. The fact that the central courts adopted the jury as their ordinary mode of proof strengthened their popularity because there was widespread dissatisfaction with the other, more primitive judicial techniques such as unilateral ordeals and trial by battle. The success of the central courts went hand in hand with the triumph of the jury and the decline, and even partial disappearance of ordeals, combat and compurgation. It meant the victory of a reasoned, rational mode of proof over the old irrational appeals to God or the obscure forces of nature.

The change was not confined to England. It was part and parcel of a general movement, a fundamental change in outlook that took place everywhere in the western world, though not everywhere at the same time or in the same way. Legal historians and ethnologists discovered long ago that there are two different attitudes towards the question of proof. There is a primitive, archaic system in which human enquiry, critical examination and reasoning play a small rôle, and where the courts are more eager to interrogate the elements of nature, such as water and fire, or spirits or divine beings, in order to elucidate the difficult question of guilt or innocence, right or wrong. We might call it the irrational approach – the term 'primitive' is now under a cloud in spite of the consecration it received in Lévy-Bruhl's famous *La Mentalité Primitive,* but terminology goes through fashions, as we all know. This irrational, 'animist' approach asks, and appears to obtain, signs from above, which are sometimes authoritatively interpreted by priests, and accepted by the courts. We find this approach in innumerable varieties among archaic people at the present time and also in the earliest stages of most developed civilizations – traces of ordeals have, for example, been detected in early Roman history. The other approach, which we might call rational, puts the burden squarely on the human mind and forces the courts to solve the riddle by all the means of enquiry and reasoning at the disposal of human intelligence; interrogation of witnesses, direct observation, indirect information, examination of written documents, confessions, deductions from various indications and traces, the result of post-mortems and so on.[2] In Europe these two very different attitudes have held sway successively, the twelfth century being the dividing line. Until then, during the first, archaic Middle Ages, irrational proof was widespread and supported by the great authorities in Church and State – Charlemagne categorically forbade any doubts about ordeals; from the twelfth century onwards they were on the decline and eventually disappeared. This distinction holds good even though some rational modes of proof existed in the first period (such as charters, instrumental witnesses and the royal sworn inquest), and relics of the old methods (such as the *purgatio canonica* and the occasional judicial combat, so popular in the feudal courts of the knightly class) continued into the second period.[3]

When we turn to England, we find that until the twelfth century the archaic modes of proof were an important and regular aspect of court activity. There was, for example, the ordeal of cold water. The person who was submitted to this 'exam', usually the accused party who had to prove his innocence, was let down in the water and carefully watched. If he sank, i.e. if the pure element of water accepted him, his innocence was established. This trial might take place in one of those ordeal-pits which one comes across in old charters, since they were a source of monastic income and were mentioned together with other elements of the patrimony of churches; we also find them in the Pipe Roll of 1166, being blessed by local clergy in connection with the Assize of Clarendon, where the water ordeal was prescribed: a payment of 10s. was made to two priests for blessing the ordeal-pits near St Edmund's Bury on the order of Geoffrey de Mandeville and Richard de Lucy, the itinerant royal justices mentioned in the first chapter (p. 21).[a] All those who were 'presented' by the juries, as ordained in the Assizes, were sent to the ordeal and we find the names of those who failed the test, 'qui perierunt in judicio aque', and consequently were mutilated for their felonies, listed at length. The ordeal of cold water might also be organized from a bridge over a stream or brook, as we see in old miniatures. It certainly was an impressive ceremony, accompanied by the chanting of the clergy, a sermon and mass, and no doubt constituted quite an event in the village life

[a] Pipe Roll 12 Henry II, p. 18: 'Et duobus presbyteris pro benedictione fossarum apud Sanctum Aedmundum 10 s. per breve comitis Gaufridi et Ricardi de Luci'; the account is rendered by the sheriff of Norfolk and Suffolk. Ten shillings is a considerable sum if one remembers that the daily wage of a workman was a penny and a villein and his whole family might be bought for 22s. (Poole, *Obligations of Society*, p. 14).

64

of the time. Distractions were not so plentiful as today and one imagines that there could be quite a crowd to watch an ordeal. Another 'judgment of God' was that of the hot iron. Here the person indicated by the proof-judgment had briefly to carry a hot iron. His hand was then bandaged and sealed and when later it appeared clean and healed or healing, again this was a sign of innocence. This ordeal was quite common in England, both in criminal and in civil pleas.

A special place was occupied by judicial combat. As far as we can see this was not practised in the Anglo-Saxon period and was introduced by the Normans, who were as fond of it as knights all over the Continent. The Conqueror expressly ordered that it was not to be enforced on English litigants[4] and the two nations were allowed to keep their respective customs. Norman combat typically co-existed with the English modes of proof (and other Norman varieties of irrational proof) until a new institution, the jury, took the place of the old system of evidence of both Englishmen and Normans and provided a common law of evidence for all. The absence of trial by battle before the Conquest is puzzling. Considering the relative abundance of our documentation, at least for the later centuries of the Anglo-Saxon period, it seems reasonable to argue *ex silentio* that trial by battle was in fact unknown in the old-English kingdom, at least in those periods where the sources are abundant – we can, of course, not be so sure about the institutions of the Angles and the Saxons at the moment when they left the boats that brought them over from their continental homeland. The amazing thing is that right through the early Middle Ages judicial combat was widespread all over the Continent, where this barbaric institution had been introduced by the Germanic tribes who had overrun the Empire. Judicial combat is attested in Frankish lands as early as the sixth century,[5] Carolingian capitularies imposed it and it began to decline only in the twelfth and thirteenth centuries. We see here the limitations of the comparative argument in history. Working on a comparative basis, one would come to the conclusion that Anglo-Saxon courts must have applied judicial combat, like the rest of Europe at the time, because of the continental invaders who introduced combat into old Roman lands, because of the general similarity of cultural development in all Europe in the 'Dark Ages', because of the great similarity of the other modes of proof and because ethnologists have shown that combat is very common at the early stages of society. It was, after all, not much more than a thinly judicialized dogfight with sticks and shields between people who had a quarrel about some property or some alleged crime.

How can this absence be explained? We might conjecture that the high degree of civilization of the Anglo-Saxons led to the disappearance of this habit, which they presumably had known at some wilder stage of their history.[6] The English kingdom was well organized and so were its law courts and – although the battle of Stamford Bridge proves its military worth – it was not so military in outlook as feudal Europe, nor was its temper so violent. The king's peace was a very real shield in the Anglo-Saxon state. It is conceivable that the action of the Church led to the disappearance of the duel, although we also find priests playing a rôle in the latter.[7] After the coming of the Normans however, combat was widespread. It was perilous and its outcome unforseeable except to saints and prophets. Reginald of Durham has a story of an accused man who was to fight before royal judges and anxiously asked a monk to enquire from Godric of Finchale, the hermit, what the outcome would be, for his life and goods would be lost if he were beaten. The holy man was reassuring and prophesied a concord, which was in fact concluded.[8]

Compurgation was another hallowed institution and for a long time the primary mode of proof. Here a party confirmed his own good right or innocence under oath and was supported by a number of oath-helpers who added the weight of their oaths to his. They were not witnesses, making statements about facts or explaining what they had observed, but were firmly on one side and their oath was assertory, merely confirming the good right or the good character of kinsman or fellow villager or citizen. We can imagine that a criminal would hardly find six or twelve compurgators amongst the lawful men of his community – communities were small and people knew each other well – to confirm in front of everybody and under oath that he was an innocent man. Frightening stories circulated about the instant punishment meted out to perjurers by the devil himself.

What was the value of these primitive modes of proof? Could they have been adequate and, if not, why did they last so long? The basic condition was widespread belief in them. The psychological barrier would stop culprits and their supporters from trying the

66

ordeal or compurgation and would betray them if they did. A guilty conscience and fear might defeat them, even at the last moment, when the priest was threatening God's wrath and the saint's relics were brought in. Even that great ruffian, Reynard the Fox, thought better of it when he saw the relics being brought in upon which he was supposed to swear his innocence, lost his nerve and fled.[9] It is always difficult to know what people really believe, and medieval clerics were the first to profit from the religious hopes and fears they taught and spread. But hell was real enough to people of all walks of life. Thus we find the abbot and monks of Ely refusing money which the widow of a wicked knight brought them, because the abbot had seen his soul being carried to hell in a vision and he and his monks were frightened to touch the money of a damned man – they must have been certain of the reality of their religious representations.[b]

Reason is not the only human faculty. It is certainly one that mankind strongly developed – some will say over-developed – but there are others, which were very pronounced in primeval man. In that pre-logic stage means other than rational enquiry were used to reach the truth, more intuitive, more akin to telepathy and other phenomena which we now call parapsychological. Thus in some way irrational modes of trial may have been adequate at a given stage of development. We know little about the statistics of these archaic practices because they flourished in periods when writing was absent or rare. What we have are normative texts, prescribing or abrogating the ordeals or indicating how they were to be held; very few texts recording court practice have survived since court rolls tend to begin when ordeals disappear. Fortunately, there are exceptions. The pipe rolls were already being kept when the ordeals were still practised and, as we saw, they contain lists of names of people who were sent to the ordeal and failed. They naturally say nothing about those who succeeded in the *examen frigidae aquae* because here there was no royal income to be recorded. For statistical material about the total of ordeals at a

---

[b] E. O. Blake, *Liber Eliensis*, Camden Third Series, 92 (London, 1962), nr 119, pp. 202–3. Earl William of Warenne died in 1080 at Lewes of wounds received at the siege of Pevensey and in the night the abbot of Ely heard his cries for help as his soul was carried to hell. The widow offered 100s. for his salvation but the abbot and his monks did not dare accept the money, as they felt it was 'not safe to possess the money of a damned man'.

given place and the proportion of successes and failures, we have to turn to another, most remarkable document, a judicial register which the clergy of the Hungarian basilica of Nagyvarad, now Oradea in Rumania, kept under King Andrew II (1205–1235). It was the habit of Hungarian law courts to send people who had to undergo the ordeal of the hot iron to Nagyvarad, or to Esztergom, Arad, Buda, Eger and Kalocsa, where other churches administered this ordeal. As well as much incidental information on practical arrangements, this *Registrum Varadiense* contains some unique numerical details.[10] Between 1208 and 1235 we find 389 cases registered, with names of suspects, details of crimes and names of judges. The yearly figures vary considerably, from 4 or 7 in 1208 and 1235, to as many as 60 and 63 in 1219 and 1213 respectively. The cases are criminal or civil, many concerning accusations of poisoning or theft. The results in these 389 cases – or rather 308, for a considerable number are incomplete or obscure – were as follows: a verdict of innocent in 130, guilty in 78, a concord reached in 75 and complaint withdrawn in 25.[11]

The clergy played a rôle in the administration of the ordeals, even in judicial combat, where the weapons were blessed and God's mercy implored.[12] Numerous *ordines* have survived. The oldest from England, including some in the vernacular, go back to the ninth century. They bear titles such as *Exorcismus aquae ad judicium Dei demonstrandum, Adiuratio ferri vel aquae ferventis, Benedictio quando judicium exituri sunt homines, Benedictio ferri ab episcopo danda,* or *Ordo judicii quo rei aut innoxii probantur ferro candenti*.[13] Numerous continental rituals have also survived and there is often a literal correspondence between them and the English ones. The *ordines* contain appropriate allusions to biblical events, such as the saving of the three boys from the fire under Nebuchadnezzar.[14] The Church christianized the ordeals introduced by the barbarians, as she christianized so many of their customs, festivals or ancient places of worship, of which she really disapproved, but found ineradicable.

This hallowed system of proof came under criticism and was fatally attacked from many quarters and in many countries in Europe in the twelfth century. The underlying reason was presumably a fairly general crisis of faith in its efficiency and justification. The same ordeals which the Church had blessed and administered for centuries were now exposed as diabolical practices by theologians, who said that it was 'tempting God' to demand constant miracles, even for the sake of saving innocent suspects. They fought these *tentamenta diabolica* vigorously and decided that they had to be 'exterminated' by Holy Church. They quoted the words of St Augustine 'Nemo debet tentare Deum, quando habet ex humana ratione quid faciat' and the Scriptures 'Thou shalt not tempt the Lord thy God'.[15] Scholars and clergymen who used to write such fine liturgies for the ordeals now sharpened their pens to ridicule them. Peter the Chanter, a famous figure in the Parisian schools of the late twelfth century, could only see tricks and cheating in them: he knew a man who, before he had to undergo the water ordeal, learnt through patient exercise how to control his breathing so as to succeed in the trial. And as far as the ordeal of hot iron was concerned, it was clear that 'innocence was too closely connected with calluses'.[16] The canonists wavered and hesitated all through the twelfth century, until the Fourth Lateran Council gave a clear and authoritative judgment. The Romanists, however, hardly ever mentioned the old proofs, and had icy and silent contempt for those barbarous devices, which are, of course, unheard of in the *Corpus Juris Civilis*.[17] Kings and other rulers objected to them, because they allowed criminals to go scot-free in an age when kings and princes began to enforce state prosecution of crime, until then often left to private initiative. Eadmer tells us that shortly before 1100, under William Rufus, fifty men were accused of breaking the forest laws and sent to the ordeal of the hot iron, but all came through unhurt and had to be considered innocent. It is hard to guess who, or what was behind this surprising collective success. Much in the ordeal of the hot iron depended on the clergy and they may have been inclined not to be too strict when forest offences were concerned (in the twelfth century some authors interpreted the successful ordeal of a known criminal as a measure of grace: God wanted to give the criminal another chance or to reward those who had confessed their sins to a priest and were then 'salvati per confessionis virtutem').[18] Whatever the reason may have been in Eadmer's story, the king was far from convinced of the innocence of the fifty men; he suspected that the clergy, who had organized the ordeal, was behind this massive acquittal, and swore that he would not be taken in again.[19] In the Assize of Clarendon of 1166 and the Assize of Northampton of 1176, Henry II prescribed that people who had been accused of serious crime[20] and had been successful

69

in the ordeal of water (and should therefore have been considered innocent),[21] were nevertheless to be banished from England, if many lawful men[22] had publicly declared them to be of bad repute – so much for Henry II's belief in the efficacy of ordeals as proof of innocence! It is clear that such kings were no longer prepared to let these dubious practices stand between them and the punishment of criminals. Townspeople also had reasons of their own for distrusting and disliking ordeals and combat, and were trying to get rid of them. Ordeals could be painful and there was a tinge of serfdom about them. Judicial combat obviously favoured the knights and the rich who could afford the best champions. By the end of the eleventh century the merchant gild of Saint-Omer, a thriving port in the south of the county of Flanders, situated on the estuary of the river Aa, had formed a system of mutual assistance to allow the brethren to hire the best champions in case one of them got involved in combat.[23] In 1116 the burgesses of Ypres, another important Flemish town, obtained a charter from Count Baldwin VII abolishing ordeals and trial by battle in their town and replacing them by wager of law. This is the oldest Flemish borough charter of which the written text (as opposed to some later confirmation of an oral grant) has survived and a very early example of the 'liberation' of a town from ordeals.[24] Thus mounting distrust, criticism and downright hostility led to the gradual disappearance of these old modes of proof. The prohibition against the clergy taking part in their administration, issued at the Fourth Lateran Council, was one factor in their downfall, although it was not applied everywhere at once. Generally speaking, Italy and the more western countries – England and Normandy, Flanders, France – were the spearhead of the movement, central Europe was slower and eastern Europe often did not follow suit until the fourteenth century.[25]

The question was how the void left by the decay of the old system was to be filled. Charter evidence, however reliable, could not fill the gap, because the time had not yet come when deeds would be drawn up for every transaction of any importance and they were in any case of little use when it came to dealing with disseisins and more serious trespasses and crimes. Other means had to be found. Generally speaking, European countries went about this task in two ways. On the one hand there were the rules and methods of evidence worked out by civilists and canonists. Their learned Romano-canonical procedure, created in the second half of the

70

twelfth and in the thirteenth century, conquered continental courts and stamped their civil and criminal procedure. Its main elements were the single judge or body of judges, who decided at the same time on questions of fact and on questions of law, who led the inquest, carried out interrogations in person or through commissioners and gave final judgment. In the field of evidence we note the use of party witnesses, confessions, secret hearings and torture.

In various other countries another system emerged. It also broke with the old irrational proofs and relied on human knowledge, insight and enquiry, but was based on a different approach and worked along different lines. We mean, of course, the jury system in all its variations. Here the trial was based on two distinct bodies, the judges who led it and eventually gave judgment, and the members of the jury who pronounced a verdict on the crucial issue of right and wrong, guilty or innocent. The voice of the vicinity, the 'truth of the land', was heard under the guidance of the judges, but was binding upon them. It was as binding, in fact, as the ordeals had been, the *vox populi* had simply taken the place of the final and inscrutable *vox Dei*. The jury could hear evidence and draw upon its own first-hand knowledge of the facts. Later it developed into a trial jury, deciding merely on the evidence put before it. Some form of jury procedure was used in the twelfth and later centuries in several lands, such as Sweden, the Low Countries and northern France, but on the Continent it gave way sooner or later to the learned Romano-canonical procedure where it had no place. Learned lawyers had nothing but contempt for the 'voice of the land'. They felt, in the graphic words of Professor Joüon des Longrais, that it was 'unheard of, scandalous and frankly barbaric that one could, even for one moment, put on the same footing the ignorant and those who had trained themselves all their lives through the learned discussions of the school'.[26] Normandy was, of course, the French province where the jury had most solidly taken root, as we can see from the thirteenth-century *coutumiers*. Recognitions survived the attack of French royal procedure based on the Romano-canonical model until the end of the thirteenth century, and we meet some survivals as late as the sixteenth: cut off from their Anglo-Norman royal support and sunk to the level of a provincial anomaly, they died a natural death.[27]

In England the jury was from the start at the heart of the Common Law and remained there. Juries consisting of men of the county, hundred or manor had been known for some time and people were paying for the privilege of having recognitions rather than the old, uncertain trials. As so often, the pipe rolls tell a striking story. Payments *pro recognitione*, with or without further specifications, appear for the first time and in very small numbers in the years 1168–70. They then vanish, but only to come back in considerable strength in the years 1175–7 and from 1179 onwards they are there for good. The first specifications we find are rather vague, like *de dote, de morte avie sue, de morte patris*; later the standard names like *de morte antecessoris, de nova dissaisina* are used. The payments were clearly made for recognitions before the royal justices, for their numbers correspond with the general eyres (i.e. 1166, 1168–70, 1175 onwards), and also with the assizes of Henry II which the eyres enforced, i.e. the Assize of Clarendon enforced in 1166 and following years, the Assize of Northampton of 1176, the Assize of Windsor and the Assize on novel disseisins, of which the results can be seen in two waves in the pipe rolls. Falling prices *pro recognitione* went hand in hand with growing numbers. The minimum of half a mark was already reached in 1179 (in 1180 we find the highest number of payments on record for the whole reign, i.e. twenty-seven) and by 1181 payments of one mark of silver were the majority – in 1175 it was still as much as ten marks.[28] Royal writs with the order 'recognosci facias', 'hold a recognition', were familiar documents.[29]

When Henry II and his councillors had to decide what mode of proof to use in their sweeping measures in the 1160s, their choice fell on the recognition, and in all the subsequent expansion of the central courts this mode of proof was conserved and developed. *Assisa venit recognitura* is the great refrain on the early assize rolls.[30] The verdict of the jury was decisive in the petty assizes, as we saw in the previous chapter, and also whenever a defendant in an action of right claimed it under the Grand Assize, to which I shall return later. The jury was called on to indict and – later – to convict suspects in criminal proceedings, and in many other circumstances. The decision of Henry's day was as understandable as it was momentous. The jury was more reliable, acceptable and reasonable than the ordeals and did not hurt the feelings of the English population as did trial by battle. On the other hand the triumph of the recognitions which greatly reduced the rôle of the typically Norman duel, did not do so in favour of a typically English mode of proof, for the jury was neither exclusively Norman nor English. Thus neither of the ethnic groups, who preferred different modes of proof, could feel disparaged. The jury had the advantage of being a well known, although not yet generalized, institution. Nor can we see an alternative. The Romano-canonical procedure was itself still in its infancy and had not even conquered the ecclesiastical courts yet, although such institutions as the interrogation of party witnesses were occasionally applied. The jury was the obvious answer and, streamlined and stereotyped, was adopted for good.

It was adopted, but not invented. For it was already an old institution in Henry Plantagenet's day, so old that its origin is a much debated historical problem. We could take as our starting point the 'Brunner thesis'. Heinrich Brunner's *Entstehung der Schwurgerichte*, which appeared a century ago, made a lasting impact and was in a different class from preceding works and their hazy ideas about the jury as originating in the primeval Teutonic forests, wherever they may have been. To talk of 'Brunner's speculations'[31] is unjustified, but it is not the only example of the animosity surrounding the treatment of this problem: for Brunner's book, packed with all the best of nineteenth-century German erudition – a formidable, continental monster – snatched away from the English that most English treasure of all, the jury, and traced its origin back to the Carolingian *inquisitio*. This most English and time-hallowed palladium of freedom was traced back to a practice of fiscal inquisitions of royal, Frankish origin introduced by the Norman conquerors. The jury was thus exposed as being originally an authoritarian and unpopular technique of administrative enquiry of continental, despotic origin and used mainly for fiscal purposes, extended later, again by royal decision, to certain types of pleas and so at last put at the disposal of all free men.

The royal inquest or *inquisitio* was indeed a well documented technique of enquiry in the Kingdom of the Franks, appearing under Charlemagne and best known in the reign of his son, Louis the Pious. In principle a royal mode of enquiry, it was used to establish the rights of the crown in land, but the king also granted its use to other persons and to churches. It was not only used in the court of the royal palace or by the *missi dominici*, but by the officials of the crown in the local courts throughout the realm, in causes concerning those who were entitled to it. Never a current and normal procedure, it deviated strongly from established practice. It was very different, of course, from ordeals of all sorts, but also from compurgation and from the use of party witnesses, who confirmed the truth of the claim of their side. In the *inquisitio* the king, the *missi*, the count of the *pagus* or some other official ordered a certain number of people whom they chose from the neighbourhood, to swear an oath and then interrogated them on some particular question; sometimes the jurors were ordered to go to the land under dispute and to indicate the boundaries. The Frankish monarchy knew a comparable *inquisitio* in criminal matters, a local jury of accusation, which appeared equally in ecclesiastical law.[32] In later centuries this procedure is found in various lands that had been part of the Kingdom of the Franks, as a technique of enquiry in the hands of the regional rulers who had stepped into the shoes of the Carolingians. We have every reason to believe that the Normans, after obtaining the Lower Seine area, found it there and did not hesitate to use it to ascertain their rights. And it is a fact that as soon as the Normans conquered England they began to use the *inquisitio* there to do just this – before their arrival there is no trace of anything resembling a royal inquest in England, where legal source material is so abundant. Similarly the sworn inquest on boundaries was introduced by them at a very early date in Sicily, not an old Frankish land.[33] There is every likelihood that it was indeed the Normans who introduced this useful royal technique into their newly conquered lands. Yet, it is not absolutely certain, for we have no document prior to 1066 proving the use in Normandy of the sworn inquest, indeed the earliest Norman text is not older than the decade after the Conquest.[34] This has been turned by several historians into an argument against Brunner, but it carries little weight. Indeed the poverty of the source material for early Norman history (because there was less writing than, for example, in England and because there has been more destruction) is such that the *argumentum a silentio* is simply out of the question. In comparison with the abundance of English sources – charters, writs, wills and law codes – the Norman texts before 1066 are miserably few and late: of the 234 charters in Mme Fauroux's collection, seven are older than the eleventh century, the first original amongst the ducal charters dates from 1006, and about half of those charters belong to the twenty years immediately preceding the Conquest.[35] That these documents, solemn title deeds, mainly church grants, contain no reference to the royal inquest was only to be expected. How dangerous it is to deduce from the absence of certain documents the absence of certain institutions is strikingly revealed by an observation made by Professor Yver: while the Norman Exchequer Roll of 1180 alone records about one hundred *recognitiones*, there has survived, except for the famous Black Book of Bayeux, only one single text of a writ ordering a recognition for the whole reign of Henry II in Normandy.[36]

After being used regularly as a royal prerogative, Brunner's thesis goes on, the Anglo-Norman inquest was occasionally put at the disposal of privileged parties and was ultimately turned into a mode of proof available to ordinary litigants in the royal courts by the assizes of Henry II in Normandy and in England. With many other historians I firmly believe, though not 'without question',[37] that as far as the history of the sworn royal inquest is concerned Brunner was right. However, the sworn royal inquest was not the only element in the rise of the jury. A tradition of free popular juries may have facilitated the success of the Common Law recognitions under Henry II and his successors. To this point we shall now turn. Brunner, who used English material to a lesser extent than continental, failed to take sufficient account of certain disturbing elements. For example in various Scandinavian countries we find, as soon as there is a reasonable flow of evidence, the jury in operation in the form of a sworn body of neighbours whose verdict tipped the scales in litigation. Thus too the Swedish *nämnden* around 1200 and the early jury men of Iceland and Norway – all, of course, in lands where no Frankish or Norman influence can be alleged. To this same Scandinavian world belongs furthermore the very clear c. 3 of the Wantage Code of Æthelred II (A.D. 978–1008, possibly in 997), where we find amongst other institutions of Danish law, applicable in the Five Boroughs, the principle that twelve legal thegns in each wapentake, and with them the reeve, were to come forward in the court and swear on the relics which were put into their hands that they would neither accuse any innocent person nor conceal any guilty one.[38] But for the absence of a royal command this is very similar to the Frankish criminal *inquisitio* and evidently a jury of accusation. There is no doubt that the Wantage text is a serious obstacle to anyone who would argue that the Carolingian sworn inquest is the only source of the jury and Brunner's attempt to interpret it away is unconvincing. We should, on the other hand, be careful not to deduce too much from the Wantage Code: it does

75

not show that the jury of indictment existed in English law. The stipulation of c. 3 is notably absent from the English Codes of Æthelred. Some historians who are very keen on establishing the English origin of the jury remind me of the inhabitants of the Anglo-Norman hundreds frantically trying to prove the 'Englishry' of some strange body in order to avoid the murdrum fine. Thus Mr Richardson and Professor Sayles have argued that c. 3 is really English law, introduced into the Danelaw.[39] There is no evidence for this and I am afraid we must here, with the great majority of historians, simply accept that the English Codes describe English institutions and the Wantage Code Danish institutions, which does, of course, not exclude the possibility that the latter could spread to regions of English law.

Equally disturbing is the fact, overlooked by Brunner, that we find in England, well before the assizes of Henry allegedly put the recognition at the disposal of litigants, the use of juries in local courts without royal intervention, purely on the basis of a party agreement to resort to that particular mode of proof. We find this even in Church courts. The cases are clear and they show juries operating in ordinary civil litigation outside the framework of the royal inquests. Here are a few cases. About 1103(?) Henry I commanded that the monks of Durham should have the land which they had deraigned in the king's court against Fulco de Lusors 'sicut homines juraverunt de comitatu'.[40] In 1133 in the chapter court of Hereford Cathedral in a trial on land 'the oath of twelve honest men and the judgment of that court' intervened to secure the land of Blackmarston for one Bernard.[41] In 1150 Hugh fitz Richard claimed part of the land and wood of Rowington against Ingulf, a monk of Reading and custos of Rowington, who obtained that a sworn perambulation of the boundaries by men selected by the two parties should take place; this was done and Hugh quit-claimed the land.[42] From about the same time comes the story of a recognition in a hallmoot, where the nuns of Godstow deraigned certain lands.[43] At the latest in 1161–2 a dispute broke out between Walter, prior of the Augustinian priory of Southwick or Porchester, and Herbert de Burhunt about certain lands which had been exchanged and which Herbert had, perhaps unjustly, enclosed. A great number of people, the justice of the Lord of Porchester, neighbours and friends, met and – all this is very reminiscent of the *Ramsey* versus *Thorney* case, described below – Herbert proposed

76

that the boundaries should be recognized by the oath of legal men of the neighbourhood. A jury was eventually composed, the prior elected four from the men of Alexander, the son of Herbert (who had died in the meantime) and Alexander elected four of the prior's men and together they elected another two men. Those ten 'juraverunt quod veritatem dicerent' and 'per sacramentum istorum recognitum est . . .' and our charter proceeds to give the details of the boundaries as they were recognized ('recognitum est per legitimos vicinos et juratores').[44] All these data point to a certain tradition of settling land litigation and fixing boundaries by the verdict of a local jury, freely resorted to by the parties. What is more, it can be shown that this tradition is older than the arrival of the Normans.

I drew attention a few years ago to the case of Ramsey Abbey versus Thorney Abbey in the reign of Edward the Confessor, probably in 1053-5, i.e. about three generations after their foundation.[45] The documents come from cartularies of both litigants and from a Ramsey chronicle. They tell us of a dispute between the abbeys about their respective parts of a fen, known as King's Delph, situated between Ramsey and the Thorney manor of Whittlesey. On the initiative of the litigants the case was decided by a jury of inhabitants of the area. After Abbot Ælfwine of Ramsey had stated his claim, five old laymen, whose names are given (two selected by Thorney and three by Ramsey), gave their sworn verdict that two-thirds of the land in question belonged to Ramsey and one-third to Thorney and fixed the boundaries, which are described in detail. The jurors, who settled the dispute by their sworn verdict, giving each party his due and indicating the precise boundary line, were not the oath-helpers of one of the litigants and nor were they witnesses giving evidence before a magistrate. The documents have been critically examined in great detail and accepted as valid by Miss Harmer[46] and my interpretation of their importance for the history of the jury has found a great measure of agreement, notably from Lady Stenton,[47] although unanimity – rare in learned works – was not achieved.

G. D. G. Hall has argued that the phrase 'after Abbot Ælfwine *betold* the boundary, against the abbey of Thorney' should be translated 'after the abbot proved his claim' (the translation adopted by Miss Harmer) and the five jurors not considered as a jury that settled the dispute.[48] It is difficult to follow him. *Betellan* does

77

not usually mean 'to prove a claim to something' (as Miss Harmer points out herself)[49] and we are left to ask what the jury would be doing after the abbot had proved his claim. Were two subsequent modes of proof needed? Did the abbot of Ramsey have to prove his case twice? If the abbot had really proved – how? – that certain areas belonged to his church, what else was there left to be done but to adjudicate it to him and have the whole proceeding confirmed by the king for safe measure? But if he only stated his claim and gave his arguments – and the current meaning of *betellan* is 'to speak about', 'to answer (a question or an objection)', 'to justify (one's position)', 'to excuse or to plead excuse for', 'to defend or exculpate oneself'[50] – it was normal for a jury thereupon to meet and decide who owned what and that is what the jurors did. 'They swore two thirds of the fen to Ramsey and one third to Thorney'[51] and indicated the boundaries, instead of 'merely designating areas after the propositions had been settled in some other way', as G. D. G. Hall suggests. That *betold* was later rendered as *dirationavit* is of no consequence; *dirationare* is not to prove one's case, but to obtain what one claims through judicial process, whatever the proof method,[52] and since the abbot of Ramsey won two-thirds of the land, he might well be said to have argued his claim so well (*betellan*), that he deraigned it, through the verdict of the jury.[c] Nor do I see that the uneven composition of the jury upon which the parties agreed, three men for Ramsey and two for Thorney, creates a problem: if those five happened to be the men who for some reason knew best and were trusted most, why should they not form a valid jury? The conclusion seems to be that we have here before the Conquest, on Danelaw territory, a local jury settling a dispute on land between litigants, who freely selected and agreed to it. The procedure was distinct from the royal inquest of later days, with its orders from above and its administrative or fiscal undertones.[53] But must we also conclude that Brunner was wrong and that we can forget about the Franks and the Normans and claim a purely English origin for the Common Law jury? Certainly not, for much of what Brunner demonstrated so cogently remains valid. We should realize, however, that local juries could find more than one application and that the jury used in an

---

[c] If he pleaded his case so well that the jurors gave him two-thirds of the fen, one might well consider that he proved his point, although the verdict of the jury was clearly the legally decisive element.

authoritative inquest is not quite the same as the jury used as a mode of settling litigation, freely agreed by the parties in preference to ordeal or compurgation.

A few years ago I therefore suggested the following outline of events, which has found some acceptance. The use of the jury in a royal inquest, by royal command and selected by royal officials, for administrative and incidentally judicial purposes, was introduced by the Normans, who knew this Frankish institution on the Continent. Occasionally we find the sworn inquest on royal command used in different ways and in defence of a variety of interests during the first hundred years after 1066. Then Henry II took two important steps. First, the recognitions on royal authority were given a definitive and uniform shape whereas previously the juries of neighbours had met locally, either in the ordinary courts or outside them, by command of a local magnate, a royal *familiaris* or an official (especially the sheriff). Henceforth they were always held before royal justices, whose rise was the great feature of the reign. Secondly, this powerful royal method of enquiry, once an exceptional technique used to protect royal and other privileged interests, was made available, as a matter of course, to ordinary free plaintiffs in a growing number of specified civil actions, and made generally available to all free defendants concerning the land they held. This momentous choice, made in the face of the crisis of the other modes of proof, was facilitated because the free use of juries to settle litigation at a local level had been known for a considerable time and had taken root in English life, even outside the Danelaw. I feel that the history of the royal sworn inquest, which is really what Brunner was writing about, was the most important element, but that it would be wrong to ignore the background of certain native habits, going back to Anglo-Saxon times. If it had not been for the royal inquest of continental origin, the native jury might have developed along the lines of the Swedish *nämnd*, a mode of proof completely integrated in the local courts, not a local body giving a verdict before royal emissaries.

Although Professor Turner[54] is wise in separating the study of criminal and civil juries, a brief reference to the jury of presentment is useful here, not to give a detailed or closely argued view, but only a provisional opinion on this most intricate problem. My impression is that although the case for the continuity from the Code of Wantage to the Assize of Clarendon is argued impressively by

Miss Hurnard, it is not fully proved.[55] Nor is it certain that the *juratores* in Pipe Roll 31 Henry I necessarily formed presenting juries. There are clear indications that presenting juries were operating at the level of the local courts, but they were in many ways different from the presenting juries systematically introduced by Henry II. This king had the merit of making the presenting jury before royal justices the standard technique for the prosecution *ex officio* of criminals, and not, as might easily have been the case, the prosecution by local justices. That he merely took over an old English institution seems to me doubtful, but a certain native tradition may have prepared the way for his initiative.

We have seen it so often. With Henry II's innovations the time of doubt and hesitation between numerous and very different techniques all vying with each other was over, clear-cut decisions were made, one method, one solution among several existing ones was adopted for good. We have seen the same hesitation and uncertainty over the courts, the writs of redress and now over the modes of proof – in each case Henry II brought the liberating decision. In the field of evidence he streamlined the existing recognitions and turned their use before royal justices into the essential mode of proof of the Common Law, both in civil and in criminal cases, by choosing them as the sole mode of proof in the petty assizes and the later Common Law actions. He did it also by adopting the presenting jury in the Assize of Clarendon, a lasting innovation in criminal law, from which the trial jury would spring after the disappearance of the ordeals. He did so also through the Grand Assize of Windsor, to which we will now turn our attention.

The Normans had introduced judicial combat as a mode of proof, even in civil litigation and it was the traditional practice in land litigation on the writ of right. But Henry II reduced its application considerably. It was conspicuously absent from the specific Common Law actions which covered an increasing number of incidents connected with land-owning and, together with *praecipe*, turned the process on right in feudal courts inexorably into a relic of the past. Furthermore, a lost enactment of Henry II, the Grand Assize probably promulgated in a great council meeting at Windsor in 1179, gave the defendant the choice between combat and a recognition by a jury of knights from the county. That the defendant had the right to demand a recognition constituted the first difference from the earlier practice that recognitions were agreed between the parties or ordained by special favour of a royal writ. The second difference was that the choice of a jury of knights introduced by this Assize led automatically to the transfer of a case to the royal court: the jury of knights met before royal justices. Indeed, the first thing the tenant who put himself upon the assize had to do was to purchase a *breve de pace habenda*, to stop the other party from proceeding in the feudal court where the action began. The writ was addressed to the sheriff and said: 'Prohibit N., unless battle has already been waged, from holding in his court the plea between R. and M. concerning one hide of land in such-and-such a vill, which the said R. is claiming against the aforesaid M. by my writ; because M., who is tenant, puts himself upon my assize, and seeks a recognition to determine which of them has the greater right in the land.'

That the Assize of Windsor was popular is clear from numerous payments *pro recognitione habenda* in the pipe rolls (see p. 72). A recognition, especially before royal justices, was a boon, for it was more rational than the other current means of proof and the royal justices could be relied on to conduct the case and execute the judgment with greater force and efficiency than most local tribunals. Thus the common man was better protected. Glanvill did not exaggerate when he wrote, about ten years after the assize was issued:

'This assize is a royal benefit granted to the people by the goodness of the king acting on the advice of his magnates. It takes account so effectively of both human life and integrity of status that all men may preserve the rights which they have in any free tenement, while avoiding the doubtful outcome of battle. In this way too, they may avoid the greatest of all punishments, unexpected and untimely death, or at least the reproach of the perpetual disgrace which follows that distressed and shameful word which sounds so dishonourably from the mouth of the vanquished [i.e. begging for mercy]. This legal constitution is based above all on equity and justice, which is seldom arrived at by battle even after many and long delays [a criticism of the feudal courts], is more easily and quickly attained through its use. Fewer essoins are allowed in the assize than in battle, and so people generally are saved trouble and the poor are saved money. Moreover, in proportion as the testimony of several suitable witnesses in judicial proceedings outweighs that of one man [a champion was by a legal fiction considered to be a witness to his employer's good right] so this constitution relies more on equity than does battle; for whereas battle is fought on the testimony of one witness, this constitution requires the oaths of twelve men.'[56]

Glanvill's remarks are clear and revealing. The Grand Assize was humanitarian and based on consideration for ordinary people and on equity. The jury avoids loss of life, its procedure is shorter and cheaper, and what twelve knights confirm under oath carries more weight than the word of one man, usually a hired champion and not a witness. It was also more efficient, for, as Glanvill contemptuously remarks, the outcome of the old mode of proof was 'doubtful' and 'justice was seldom arrived at by battle', a devastating pronouncement on an institution that was supposed to prove where right and wrong lay, especially as it came from a man who had lived through many years of judicial activity and was not in the habit of going around with his eyes and ears shut.

In the Duchy of Normandy the course of events followed a similar pattern. Here too we find the decline of the archaic modes of proof and their replacement by ducal recognitions (*requenoissants*). The latter were introduced with the ducal writs of the novel disseisin type, which we met in the previous chapter, and in all probability also by a general enactment comparable to the English Grand Assize.[57] The pattern of judicial organization was also very similar. We find the traditional local courts, whether feudal or viscontiel, in decline and the ducal itinerant justices, whom we meet occasionally under Henry I, on the ascendant under Henry II, touring the duchy, taking the local recognitions and administering ducal justice – they were known as the *Magna Assisia*. The permanent centre was the Norman Exchequer, where the duke or his seneschal or *capitalis justiciarius* sat to do justice.[d] Here as in

[d] R. Besnier, 'Action et juridiction à l'époque des coutumiers normands', *Tijdschr. v. Rechtsgeschiedenis,* 17 (1941), 1–18. The conquest of the duchy by the King of France led to great changes. The seneschal disappeared and so did the itinerant justices, who were replaced as ordinary judges by regional *grands baillis*. The Norman modes of proof were eroded in the course of the thirteenth century (as was the pleading by ducal writs) and replaced by Romano-canonical techniques. The jurymen were considered as an inferior sort of witnesses (*de credentia,* as opposed to witnesses *de scientia*) and they were subjected as party witnesses to individual interrogation by the judge, see Besnier, 'La dégénérescence', pp. 48–61, and Strayer, 'The writ of Novel disseisin in Normandy', pp. 3–12.

England, the recognitions had started as exceptional techniques of enquiry, applied by the duke to his own rights or bestowed by him on privileged plaintiffs.

Historians have tried to establish when the recognitions organized by the duke or his justices became a 'boon granted to the people' – to use Glanvill's words. Haskins made a great effort to elucidate this question in spite of the extreme dearth of documents. He concluded, against Brunner and quite rightly, that the *secundum assisiam meam* in two documents of Geoffrey Plantagenet and one of Henry II (the latter from A.D. 1156) was insufficient grounds for the assumption that the recognitions had at that early stage been put generally at the disposal of litigants, since it might easily refer to decisions taken in individual cases.[58] He thought, however, that the suit of William, son of Théion de Fonte, who in 1159 unsuccessfully claimed the meadow of Bapeaume against the monks of St Stephen in Caen, proved that at that early date plaintiffs could demand the use of sworn inquests in Normandy. He interpreted the phrase 'defecit se de iure et de consideratione recti coram Roberto et coram baronibus Normannie in curia regis et de assisia quam inde requisierat' as meaning 'William ... who claimed the right to them, failed as regards his claim and the decision of right before Robert and the barons of Normandy in the king's *curia* and as regards the assize which he had demanded with respect thereto'.[59] This interpretation cannot be accepted. *Se deficere* does not mean 'to fail', but 'to give up a claim, to quitclaim'; nor does *requirere* necessarily mean 'to demand', it can also mean 'to ask', so that William may merely have asked for the privilege of having a recognition; and last but not least, *assisia* has so many meanings that we cannot possibly be sure that *assisia* meant a sworn inquest and not, for example a 'sitting of a court' in which case we would translate 'William ... gave up his claim ... and the meeting of the court which he had asked'.[60]

Henry II's early years in Normandy are obscure and we greatly miss the relative abundance of the English sources of the period. Ducal enactments are known to have been made in Normandy, but no texts comparable to the English Constitutions and Assizes of Henry II are conserved.[61] For Norman law-books we must wait till the first years of the thirteenth century and there is nothing comparable to the impressive series of English pipe rolls: all we have for the twelfth century from the Norman Exchequer is a fragment of the roll of 1184 and the rolls of 1180 and 1195.[62] The only certainty we have is that by 1180 recognitions were very commonly used, for the Exchequer Roll of that year is full of them. However a precise chronology of their introduction in the earlier part of Henry II's reign will probably elude us forever, and make vain the discussion about English or Norman priority in the establishment of the new system, based on writs and recognitions, as a common and ordinary procedure.

What is clear is that Henry II's steps in the field of evidence gave England and Normandy a most advanced system, much ahead of the Continent. When in later times most of Europe, including Normandy, adopted the Romano-canonical procedure, the English system began to look quaint and antiquated. Later again, the disadvantages of the oppressive continental procedure, with its absence of any popular element, aroused criticism and opposition and the jury was seen as a safeguard against injustice and as a procedure worthy of free men. It was therefore introduced or reintroduced on the Continent where a good many of its origins had lain many centuries before. We have here one of these cycles which historians are always amused to discover. There are moments when archaic uses suddenly appear to have a value that nobody suspected and to offer advantages that were hidden for a long time. And with this thought on – shall we say 'the importance of being archaic' – I should like to end this chapter.

4

English law and the Continent
'Nolumus leges Angliae mutari'

Let us start this chapter with a paradox in spite of the fact that
'relish for paradox has no place in sober history'.[1] It is that English
and continental law irrevocably took their different courses in the
very century, the twelfth, when English civilization was closer to
the Continent and less insular than at any other time. The Common
Law and the 'Romano-Germanic family', two of the systems of
universal significance analysed in David's *Grands systèmes de droit
contemporains*,[2] are both of European origin, yet they differ greatly.
To lawyers outside Anglo-Saxon lands the traditional Common Law
is well nigh incomprehensible – Bentham spoke of its 'incognosci-
bility' – because there are no codes that encompass it, a circum-
stance that turned away the Japanese under the great modernizer
Meiji, in favour of continental codes. But Englishmen fully share
this incomprehension mixed with aversion, as far as 'the alien
jungle of the *Code Civil*' is concerned – I quote the phrase used by
a B.B.C. correspondent, in a programme on the legal consequences
of Britain joining the European Common Market.

Why is the Common Law so different from the law of the European Continent? Why above all did this national law of England
enter upon its different course precisely in the twelfth century?
English scholars studied then in continental universities, John of
Salisbury was bishop of Chartres and Nicholas Breakspear became
Pope Adrian IV, the English Church was ruled by clerics of continental extraction and very attentive to papal directives.[3] The
knightly class that colonized England was of continental extraction
and owned land on both sides of the Channel. Kings, prelates and
knights spoke French and the kingdom itself was no more than an
acquisition first of the Norman and then of the Angevin family. A
glorious acquisition, no doubt, but not one that outshone the other
windfalls of the Plantagenets – Normandy and Aquitaine. The Kingdom of England lived in symbiosis with the Angevin possessions on
the Continent, and was not the centre of their vast conglomerate.
It is good to remember that Richard I spent no more than six

months of his ten years' reign in England and that it was not by its own choice that the French family, to which he belonged, eventually lost its homelands and had to be content with England and some other conquests in the British Isles.[a]

To the simple question 'why is English law so different?', some people have given the simple and at first sight obvious answer: 'because English people are so different'. This sort of answer had a particular appeal for nineteenth-century romantic scholars, especially in Germany, who saw the *Volksgeist* at work in all the manifestations of human culture. The heavy hand of Hegel is tangible here. There is no need to expatiate on the conceptions of the great German philosopher, but the following attractive and imaginative description has been given by Professor Gombrich of Hegel's vision of the 'national spirit':

'I like to picture the content of this all important paragraph [in the *Vorlesungen über die Philosophie der Geschichte*[4]] diagrammatically as a wheel from the hub of which there radiate eight spokes. These spokes represent the various concrete manifestations of the national spirit . . . They are the nation's religion, constitution, morality, law, customs, science, art and technology. These manifestations which are visible on the periphery of my wheel must all be understood in their individual character as the realizations of the *Volksgeist*: they all point to a common centre. In other words, from whichever part on the outside of the wheel you start moving inward in search of their essence, you must ultimately come to the same central point. If you do not, if the science of a people appears to you to manifest a different principle from that manifested in its legal system, you must have lost your way somewhere.'[5]

Thus the legal system of a people must be the manifestation of some

---

[a] J. Le Patourel, 'The Plantagenet Dominions', *History*, 50 (1965), 289–308: the Angevin succession was continuous in the male line, father to eldest surviving son, from Fulk 'le Réchin' to Richard I; a family enterprise whose greatest plums were England and Aquitaine. J. Le Patourel, 'The Norman Succession, 996–1135', *Eng. Hist. Rev.* 86 (1971), 225–50, shows that the Conqueror had not really desired the separation of England and Normandy which followed upon his death and that a real unification, as opposed to a merely personal one, would have been quite normal; the same general theme was developed by the same author in the Stenton Lecture 1970 under the title *Normandy and England 1066–1144* (Reading, 1971).

central principle, which you will also find in its science, religion etc.[6] These ideas are interesting but are they helpful to the historian? Do we really explain the course of events by blaming or praising the national character or the 'national spirit', a vague and pliable entity,[7] for producing a given legal system, or are we playing with words? 'National character, the genius of a people,' said Maitland, 'is a wonder-working spirit which stands at the beck and call of every historian,'[8] and C. K. Allen has reminded us that 'law is seldom of pure-blooded stock' and 'national' is a dangerous word to use, without qualification, of almost any legal institution.[9] It is possible that national character, a vague but nevertheless real thing – that the Normans were different in type from the English is clear enough – may just as well be a product of the legal system as the other way round. There is little doubt that living for centuries under the Common Law must have produced many 'Anglo-Saxon attitudes'. In fact England might be considered a textbook example of the importance of a legal system in the moulding of a nation's character.[10] Moreover, if national character is the fountain of the Common Law, why did the latter enter its historical path in the least English phase of English history and why should a similar system have originated at the same time, as we have seen, in Normandy?

If the national character does not help us – and I shall come back to this point later – then maybe the climate could offer an explanation. But with due respect for the peculiarities of English summers and winters and the severity of their impact on people's lives, I feel that this old favourite of social explanation was neatly disposed of by Hegel's striking and unanswerable phrase 'wo einst die Griechen waren, sind jetzt die Türken'. The wonderful skies and the marvellous coastline of Hellas have failed to elicit any repetition of the Greek miracle among the later inhabitants of those blessed shores.

Shall we have better luck, in our search for 'interpretations of legal history',[11] by turning to the powerful economic factor? It seems unlikely, for twelfth-century England (and Normandy) where the Common Law was born, was not strikingly different. Neither her agricultural economy, with the manorial system dominating in some areas and small freeholders in others, nor her developing towns and expanding money economy were unique in Europe. Let us therefore give up this sociologist's chase for some general factor and do the proper work of a historian by studying the precise and particular circumstances in which the Common Law arose, without forgetting some that were not less important because they were fortuitous.

The Common Law of England – so different from the *jus commune* or common learned law of the European universities – is the oldest national law in Europe. It is the oldest body of law that was common to a whole kingdom and administered by a central court with a nation-wide competence in first instance. In the rest of Europe, the law was either European or local, not national. In consequence a number of countries paradoxically adopted the cosmopolitan *jus commune* to provide a national legal system which the divergent customs could not produce, because they were not sophisticated enough and regional pride resisted the imposition of the customs of one region on all others (as, nowadays, European laws and languages serve as common, national tools in various African countries beside the native customs and dialects). German legal unification through the introduction of the *jus commune* was not completely successful and in France legal unification was not reached until the Civil Code of 1804.

For centuries, in fact until the Judicature Acts of 1873 and 1875, this Common Law of England consisted of a system of actions or legal remedies, each commanding its own procedure, whereas continental law knew general procedural rules which governed all or large classes of causes.[12] English law prefers precedent as a basis for judgments, and moves empirically from case to case, from one reality to another. Continental law tends to move more theoretically by deductive reasoning, basing judgments on abstract principles; it is more conceptual, more scholastic and works more with definitions and distinctions. In other words it was moulded by the Roman Law of the medieval universities. It was this professors' law, marked by exegesis and commentaries on learned books and glosses, which made continental law different from the Germanic and feudal customs and laws of England. With the exception of Bracton's great law-book, we find none of it in the Common Law, where the Year Books, with their reports of court cases, were typical and utterly different from William Durand's systematic *Speculum Judiciale*. In England lawyers received their training in the Inns of Court, technical colleges where they learnt their craft like every medieval craftsman, in contact with practising masters, not in universities at the feet of scholars who were apt to lose themselves in controversy. English law worked essentially within the existing feudal framework, whereas continental law incorporated a vast amount of extraneous elements, mainly of Roman origin. Consequently the feudal idea of relation was central in English, and the Roman idea of will in continental law.[13] A final difference is the absence of codification in England. The tradition of case law and empiricism makes very poor soil for codification – the Romans, who were first and foremost practical jurists, never had a codification – but with systematic theory and logical deduction from general premises, codes came naturally on the Continent.[14]

These and other differences are clear and familiar enough to every lawyer interested in comparative studies. Has this difference between England and the Continent been there ever since the *gens Anglorum* entered on the scene of history? If not, at what juncture did the parting of the roads take place? We can answer at once that the difference was not inborn, lying between English law of all periods and continental law of all periods, but exists only between the English Common Law and the continental law of the later Middle Ages, both of which took their distinct course in the twelfth century. There was no essential, inherent difference from the start. It came about at a later stage, when a decisive new phase was entered by both England and the Continent, but in opposing ways. During the archaic 'first feudal age' there was no essential difference in the legal landscape of customary law, largely unwritten and strongly Germanic, administered in local courts in a way that strikes us as primitive and irrational – after 1066 even feudalism became common to England and the Continent.

The breach came with the momentous modernization of European society in general, and the law in particular, that took place in the twelfth and thirteenth centuries, a watershed of the greatest importance. In all Europe there was a break with the old post-Carolingian world and a process began which led eventually to the sovereign national states of modern times, with their central bureaucracy, rational approach and modernized law. The towns in many lands broke with the old order, the universities rose and with them the study of Justinian's *Corpus Juris Civilis*. Monarchical government made great strides forward, the rulers of France undertook the unification of the kingdom and created in the Parliament of

Paris a central high court, occupied by professional jurists educated in the universities. Politically speaking, feudalism had spent its force and vast new monetary resources allowed the state to employ non-feudal officials of a type that had all but disappeared since the collapse of the Roman and Frankish empires.

Though this vast surge forward happened everywhere, it did not take place everywhere at the same time. It was also different in intensity and stress. Thus in some countries decisive measures were taken before Roman law exercised any profound influence, in others the innovation in legal life was roughly parallel to the revival of Roman law. In still others it took place long after medieval Roman law had become a mature and established system. Chronology is of the utmost importance here – and it is not superfluous to stress this elemental ingredient of history. The breakthrough of a centralized and modernized legal system took place exceptionally early in England (and Normandy), before Roman law was in a position to exert any profound influence. In Europe no other royal court was accessible to all free men in the twelfth century; the Paris Parliament did not emerge until the middle of the thirteenth and then, as far as ordinary people were concerned, only as a court of appeal. There is in 1188 in Europe no other book like Glanvill. We have to wait till the early thirteenth century to find something comparable in France and then only in Normandy, where the Anglo-Norman tradition was vigorous.[15] In the Kingdom of Sicily in spite of some important legislative measures in the twelfth century,[16] the first comprehensive law-book belongs to the time of Frederick II, and his *Libri Augustales* of 1231 are crammed with Roman law. In Saxony around the same time the *Sachsenspiegel* of Eike von Repgau (*c.* 1224–7) makes an archaic impression in comparison with the older work of Glanvill. Nowhere in Europe is there a national legal system that had done away to all practical intents and purposes with the archaic modes of evidence earlier than in England; nowhere do we find the practice of court enrollments as early as in England.

If the modernization of the law came exceptionally early in England, it was also remarkably systematic. The activity of the justices at Westminster and in eyre and the various actions with which they dealt formed a coherent whole and were grasped and described as such. This new law and its judicial apparatus were national and royal. Not local magnates, but the king and his central justices were the bearers of the whole system and its application was nation-wide. This was very unlike the Continent, where local and regional custom reigned supreme and even the central courts judged according to local custom in appeal cases. This modernized law of England was essentially autochthonous, based on known rule and familiar practice. It owed very little to Roman law. Glanvill betrays some acquaintance with the Institutes of Justinian, a beginner's textbook,[17] and Bracton, who wrote two generations after Glanvill, knew a good deal of Roman law, both from the *Corpus* – almost five hundred different sections of the Digest and Code are quoted – and from its commentators – Azo, Tancred and Raymond of Peñafort.[18] But Bracton, with his very real understanding of Roman law, was unrepresentative, an erratic block in the Common Law landscape. He formed no school, neither did his example find followers.

Not so on the Continent, where from the twelfth century onwards learned commentaries on the *Corpus Juris Civilis* and Romano-canonical treatises on procedure appear and, where, more important, we find from the thirteenth century onwards a continuous stream of treatises on customary law and important royal legislation, which had absorbed Roman law to various degrees. But by that time the Common Law and the Common Law courts were already firmly and unshakably established. They had taken root and received their essential techniques and outlook in the days of Henry II, before Roman law was influencing legal practice in lay courts anywhere in Europe, before the great comprehensive treatises like Azo's *Summa Codicis* (A.D. 1208–10) had appeared, and even before the ecclesiastical courts in England had gone over to the Roman-inspired procedure, which we find in the humble *ordines judiciorum* of the twelfth and in the great procedural treatises of the thirteenth century.[19] This precocity, the premature character of the rise of the Common Law is all-important. Let us not forget that the fundamental assize of novel disseisin is of 1166 at the latest.

What was there in the way of treatises and practice of the new Roman and canonical procedure in Europe at that time? The very brief *Summa de judiciis* of Bulgarus, written at the latest in 1141 in Italy, the *Summa de actionum varietatibus* of Placentinus, another Bolognese scholar, written c. 1162–5[20] and the *Ulpianus de edendo*, an Anglo-Norman work of very uncertain date:[21] these are three slim pioneering works, precursors of the great classical treatises.[22] Nor was the new fashion universally popular. Reservations were expressed in clerical circles about the new trends. It was felt that there were too many innovating decretals and too many appeals to Rome to the detriment of the Ordinary, and there were violent objections to Roman law.[23] As to the Church courts, their practice was slowly beginning to be influenced by the new Romano-canonical learning in the course of the second half of the twelfth century.[b] The ecclesiastical documents show that in England the breakthrough of the new procedure and its distinct terminology did not take place before the 1180s;[24] it is noteworthy that this coincides roughly with the rise of a class of new judicial officers, the bishops' officials.[25] The collecting of papal legislation is a good sign of interest in the new legal developments. The earliest extant English collection of decretals is the Wigorniensis Altera, certainly one of the earliest composed in England. It is conceivably as early as 1173–4, but the most recent decretals which it contains could be as recent as 1179 or 1181.[26] However, in the 1180s the Common Law was already set on its course and Glanvill's Treatise, towards the end of the decade, would greatly strengthen it. In other words, when at the turn of the twelfth century Romano-canonical learning began to conquer the practice of Europe's ecclesiastical courts and, in the course of the thirteenth century, to influence its lay courts and writers on customary law, it was too late for the Common Law to be affected in any substantial way. Even Bracton who was ready to borrow what he could, could not alter the nature of the 'Laws and Customs of England'. The Common Law was set in its own techniques, practice, ideas and institutions, had created its own framework and had produced a technical terminology of considerable sophistication and precision that was to last for centuries and constitute a barrier to civilian influence. It was so adequate for the needs and so rooted in the social reality of the time that any attempt to change it would have met with the famous 'nolumus leges Angliae mutari', with which in the Statute of Merton of 1236 the barons opposed the clergy's request to change English marriage laws.

Hardly have we, by drawing attention to the precocity of English modernization, answered one question, than another arises. Why this precocious development in England among European states? Historians are well aware of England's precocity vis-à-vis other

---

[b] We have seen, p. 82, n. 57, that in their traditional practice even such uncanonical devices as the jury were used. It took time for the novelties of the *ordines judiciarii* to replace those old fashioned usages.

European kingdoms, notably that of the Capetians, and of her pioneering rôle in what Kienast has called 'the Intensivierung des Staats-
betriebs' in the later Middle Ages.[27] No one will be simplistic
enough to explain this complex phenomenon by naming one single
cause. There must have been many, but some were more important
than others and one that we should certainly not overlook is the
achievement of old-English kingship in building a unified state.
England had learned to live as one country, under one government
with a national network of institutions, officials and courts, during
those very centuries when elsewhere the Frankish state and its successors were falling apart and their administration disintegrating.
The old-English state, unified and consolidated in the tenth and
eleventh centuries, afforded the political basis on which later generations could build the Common Law. These generations happened to
be ruled by kings of Norman and Angevin descent and their continental followers. They added their own genius as rulers and administrators and keepers of law and order, which they displayed
in their Sicilian as well as in their English conquest. They also
brought their own kind of controlled and constructive feudalism,
the kind that its Carolingian creators must have had in mind and of
which it was rightly said that 'the better feudalism works the more
rapidly it generates a political structure which is no longer completely feudal'.[28] England's Norman masters were rapacious, but
they set about their business in a systematic way that was unparal-
leled and brought existing fiscal institutions to near-perfection.
The country which was so precocious in modernizing its legal system
was also ahead of Europe in fiscal administration.[29] Again, the
Normans certainly knew how to rule over multiracial lands. In
Sicily the Latin Normans ruled over Greeks and Arabs, in England
over the native English and Danes – the latter were politically
absorbed but had retained very marked legal and social characteristics.

Twelfth-century England had a very mixed population and was
keenly aware of it – the amalgamation of the *Franci* and the *Anglici*
did not take place until the turn of the century. This raises the question of the rôle of the 'national character' in the foundation of the
Common Law. I have already mentioned the rôle of the 'national
spirit', but I would like to go into it more deeply here, because on
this question there are notions about that stand in need of some
'demythologizing'. The late Professor Pringsheim, a leading legal

historian for many years, was very interested in English law and its similarities with the classical law of Rome.[30] He lectured on the subject in Cambridge and in Oxford in 1933 and published his lecture under the significant title 'The Inner Relationship between English and Roman Law'.[31] The learned author insisted on the difference between the classical law of Rome and the late Roman or Byzantine law of the time of Justinian. Studying the similarities between the classical Roman law and the English Common Law, he showed that both differed profoundly from Byzantine Roman law and from the medieval Roman law that was based on it. The contrast is thus between classic Roman law and the Common Law on the one hand and the late Roman and continental learned law on the other.

'Continental law with which the English Common Law is usually contrasted is influenced by the law of Justinian and the classical law has influenced it only indirectly. The spirit of Roman law during its classical epoch is related to the spirit of English law; the spirit of Justinian's era is almost in opposition to the English spirit. Two pairs are in opposition, on the one side the law of the Corpus Juris and the continental system influenced by it, and on the other side the classical Roman law and the English law scarcely influenced by it, but bearing an inner relationship to it.'

Thus Pringsheim (p. 78), who then proceeded to quote a few examples, such as the Roman formulae-process and the English writ-process[32] and to point out certain dissimilarities such as the all-important rôle of precedent in English law as against the dominating position of the edict, the *responsa* and the legal treatises in Rome. All this is very illuminating. There are few more impressive and bizarre developments in history than the efforts of the Bolognese glossators to pick up the thread of Roman legal history where it had been dropped six centuries before and to bring the law of the Roman Republic and Empire to its doctrinal fulfilment and logical conclusion in the universities of medieval Italy. Yet, 'while the other nations of Western Europe were beginning to adopt the ultimate results of Roman legal history, England was unconsciously reproducing that history'.[33] It is where Pringsheim attempts to *explain* this inner relationship – this similar 'spirit', to use the phrase current since Montesquieu's *Esprit des Loix* and Jhering's

Geist des römischen Rechts – that we begin to feel doubts, for he finds the explanation in the similar character of the two nations. In a Hegelian vein he writes that the similarity between the legal systems of England and classical Rome 'is founded upon an undeniable similarity between those two peoples, a similarity of national characteristics which they have exhibited during their long history' (p. 77); 'both English and Roman law have developed independently of foreign influence, this is a consequence of the strong national character of these nations' (p. 79). Are there in Europe no other nations with a very strong national character and a legal system that differs greatly from that of classical Rome or England? Is it not pushing the desire for comparison a bit far to maintain that 'in the domain of art both nations, [i.e. Rome and England] show similar inclinations and endowments' (p. 85)? Although I feel no special desire to fight spirits and although Pringsheim sounded a warning note that 'this spirit, the fundamental character of a nation, will always remain a secret, it is not at all desirable to attack it with rational considerations' (p. 90), I feel the subject is too important to be left untouched.

The disturbing element in Pringsheim's construction is the co-existence in England in the crucial twelfth century of several national groups. There were Normans, called 'French' in the documents, and Englishmen. There were also Flemings and Welsh-men, whom the charters sometimes mention specifically, and there were the descendants of the Danes. The two essential nations, forming two distinct social classes, were the *Franci* and the *Anglici*, so familiar in the royal and private writs and charters of the eleventh and twelfth centuries.[34] These two nations – for if ever there were 'two nations' in England, it was in the century of the foundation of the Common Law – were separated by a wide gulf. The 'French' were of continental origin, ruled the country and its Church, controlled its wealth, were kept together by Anglo-Norman feudalism and held land in Normandy and in England. They spoke French[c] – even Richard I's chancellor knew no English, much to the

---

[c] This linguistic and social barrier was a serious handicap, see the story of Brictric, a parish priest who was angry with St Wulfric, a miracle-working anchorite in the days of Henry I and Stephen, because the saint had cured a dumb man who proceeded to speak English and French. On seeing this Brictric blamed the saint who had never given him, his old friend, the use of French so that 'when he came before the bishop and archdeacon he was compelled to be silent like a dumb man' (Stenton, *English Society*,

annoyance of the people[35] – were very close to continental civilization and had a military, knightly way of life. They had scant respect
for the traditional values of the conquered English, with whom
they only began to intermarry in the reign of Henry II – Richard
fitz Neal wrote (optimistically?) in 1179[36] that in his days intermarriage between French and English had become so frequent that
it was hard to distinguish them, at least, he added, if they were free
people[37] – but the whole point is that the majority of the English
were unfree *nativi*, so that the terms '_naif_', 'rustic', 'villein' and
'Englishman' were interchangeable.[d] This was the other nation, the
mainly unfree, English speaking, peasants, who were barred from
high office and led a humble life in local argriculture, saving with
difficulty such elements as they could of their own historical
treasures, their kings, their saints and their language.[38]

Whose national character then is reflected in the Common Law?
That of the Normans or that of the English? Some of its elements
were no doubt of English (and Danish?) origin: for example,
some forms of landholding and manorial organization and the
village life as it appeared in the hallmoots and hundred- and
county courts (but that was not where the Common Law dwelt);
some elements of the jury procedure and, of course, the writ (but
hardly in the form it took at Common Law). But much more was of
Norman origin and belonged to the Norman way of life. The Common Law was essentially feudal land law[39] and feudalism came
from the Continent. The sworn inquest also came from Normandy.
The typical executive writ and its judicialized successors had been
developed by Norman and Angevin kings. The royal officers and
feudatories who shaped and defined the Common Law in its formative years were overwhelmingly members of the 'French' nation,
just as Henry II Plantagenet, its founder, was himself a very French
scion of an old French dynasty.[40] Also, in spite of what Pringsheim
said (p. 80), this Common Law was the 'law of a class' and not
'of the whole kingdom and the men who dwell therein'. The
Common Law took no interest in the unfree peasants who were

pp. 211–12). As Winfield, *Chief sources*, p. 8 strikingly puts it: 'A man who
could speak English only was underbred as a courtier and half-educated as
an official.'

[d] As when in a very distant past the English had conquered Britain and
wealas, the Germanic word for the Britons, had come to mean 'slaves', so
now to the Normans who had conquered the English, *Anglicus* came to
mean villein.

harshly excluded and even amerced if they tried to use its benefits.[41]
The men who created it were members of a small dominant aristocracy and it was accessible to them and the free minority of the
natives (an upper layer amongst the English), and they created it
in order to preserve harmony among the free, landowning top class.
It is not surprising that the technical language of this 'English'
Common Law was French and remained so (though it became less
and less understandable to French people) until the seventeenth and
eighteenth centuries.[42] After all, when the foundations were being
laid, the Common Law was undistinguishable from the system of
brefs, requenoissants and tenures that grew up in Normandy at the
same time to serve the same ruler and the same class,[43] and this
legal system certainly could not be called English.[e] It was founded
in a period when 'academically, as well as in the mores of aristo-
cratic life, England was a colony of the intellectual Empire of
France'.[44] This Anglo-Norman law only became English after the
loss of Normandy, nurtured (while it withered away in Normandy)
by a state that had turned from the Anglo-Norman into an English
state, with English instead of French kings, justices of English
descent on the benches[45] and with an aristocracy that had in the end
become so 'English' that 'the Conquest was viewed with distaste by
men who were French in speech and habits, and who owned their
whole family fortune to William I and his successors'.[46] It was in the
thirteenth century that the fusion of Norman and English into one
nation took place and that Common Law, which bound together
freemen of every descent became truly English, distinct from continental law and part of the country's identity.[f] It was then seen

[e] Very few 'anti-Norman' historians are prepared to go the whole length
and to see Norman law under Henry, including the sworn inquest, as an
importation from England. None, so far as I know, has yet pretended that
feudalism was introduced from England to Normandy. The precision,
briskness and sharpness of the Common Law procedure and its whole
atmosphere are quite unlike the traditional qualities of the English of
Anglo-Saxon times, who are depicted as warm and gentle (Knowles,
'Archbishop Thomas Becket', p. 101) and prepared 'to take every opportunity of ending civil suits by compromise between the parties', a conception of law 'which prefers peaceful settlements under the authority
of a court to judicial decisions' (Stenton, *English Justice*, p. 7). If the
Common Law started geographically as an Anglo-Norman phenomenon,
its tone in that initial phase was overwhelmingly Norman, though count-
less generations of English lawyers later turned it into a very English
monument indeed.

[f] G. Dietze, *Magna Carta and Property* (Charlottesville, Va., 1965), p. 63:
'After the loss of Normandy a greater feeling of common nationality

that the Common Law offered a way out of the difference between Englishmen and Normans, held them together and solved existing contradictions.

We thus arrive at a view opposing Pringsheim's and we find that the Common Law in the thirteenth century was indeed the law of a class. It was the law of the free landowners, a class which was losing its clear Anglo-Saxon or Norman consciousness and was in need of a new national identity, which a common system of law and law courts helped to provide.[47] Thus in the thirteenth century the name of Englishman was something to be proud of,[48] whereas a century before it denoted servile status, and a system based on French feudal law, administered in French, became the pride of the English nation. The Common Law helped to create a sense of nationhood and greatness in late medieval England. It made people aware of their distinctness, as compared with the other nations in the British Isles and on the Continent. It inspired such works as Sir John Fortescue's proudly titled *De Laudibus Legum Angliae*, written in 1470 or 1471, for the instruction of the young Prince Edward, and Wycliff's attack on Roman law as 'heathen men's law' and his appeal 'from the rules imposed externally by Roman law and the pope to the rules which Englishmen made for themselves by their everyday conduct'.[49] I am tempted to turn Pringsheim's thesis upside down and to suggest – with some exaggeration though not without some justification – that the Common Law was not a consequence of the English national character, but rather one of its formative elements.

Pringsheim was neither the first nor the last to claim the English national character as the prime mover of the Common Law.[g] In

developed among the English ... Magna Carta originally mainly intended for feudal *homines*, was increasingly applied to all *liberi homines*. The feeling that Magna Carta secured freedom for all the people increased as the thirteenth century advanced.' The disengagement from Normandy and from landholding there was the traumatic experience that finally turned the English Normans into Englishmen, but it was a negative experience; Magna Carta (which has nothing to say of French or Normans) and the Common Law were positive factors. The question when the Norman conquerors stopped feeling like Normans has historical parallels. When did the English settlers in America stop feeling like Englishmen to become Americans, when did the Dutch settlers in South Africa feel they were no longer Europeans?

[g] In the seventeenth and eighteenth centuries the triumph of Parliament in England, when absolutism was victorious on the Continent, was *inter alia* explained by the national character of the English, who were 'natural

1904 Sir Frederick Pollock had made a similar claim all the more dramatic for its appeal to the divinity, replacing divinely ordained kings by a divinely ordained Common Law and he placed the latter even more out of the reach of criticism than Pringsheim's 'national spirit'. Maybe nothing less than the divinity seemed adequate to explain such a majestic thing.[50] Indeed, after pointing out, strikingly and accurately, that in the later Middle Ages 'there must have been much temptation for learned persons to regard any specially English ideas and usages as a kind of provincial heresy' (p. 57) and after speaking of the 'seeming barbarism' of the Common Law, he proceeded to explain that even so great a legislator as Edward I could not have changed the peculiar nature of English law and he gave the reason why: 'Far be it from me to say that Edward I could really have done otherwise if he would. I believe in "the divinity that shapes our ends". Rather the fact that our institutions were ordered as they were, and seemed to be so quite naturally, bears witness to the depth of national sense and tradition, a depth under a surface hardly ruffled by conscious effort' (p. 58) – thus the lofty words of Sir Frederick Pollock.[51] He may well have taken a leaf from the civilians' book, for they too considered their law as a 'gift from heaven'.[52]

That this romantic vein of legal history has not entirely dried up, may appear from the following lines, written in a colourful and flowery style, all too rare in 'the barren fields of law books': 'English law, as its history shows, was made by Englishmen for Englishmen and expresses the spirit of England.' However, it is admitted that some elements came from elsewhere: 'English law is like a river. The channel widens and deepens as it flows through the course of years and tributaries join it from time to time. It was first fed by the springs of the common law, but the fountain of equity and the wells of the law merchant and ecclesiastical law have increased the waters of the growing current. And upon the tide is borne the ship which is the soul of England.'[53] I do not know whether all this is good poetry but it looks like faulty history to me. However, I suggest that we leave these souls and spirits and these rivers, channels, springs, wells, tides and other deep waters into

asserters of liberty'. See C. Robbins, 'Why the English Parliament survived the Age of Absolutism. Some explanations offered by writers of the 17th and 18th centuries', *Studies presented to the Internat. Comm. for the Hist. of Represent. and Parl. Instit.*, 18 (Louvain, 1958), 199–213 (= Xth Internat. Cong. of Hist. Sc., Rome, 1955).

which romantic writers easily get caught and that we move on to have a look at another key element in the founding years of the Common Law, the personality of Henry II, that 'subtle inventor of new judicial forms',[54] that man of genius – the word is not too strong – who was 'by instinct a lawyer'[55] and whose judicial sense was so developed that the kings of Castile and Navarre in 1177 submitted a territorial dispute to his arbitration.

Under Henry II the Anglo-Norman complex reached its zenith and in all probability it was in the last years of his reign that 'the royal power in England was at the highest level it was to reach before the Tudor period'.[56] In those years the Common Law machinery was unshakably established and his personal drive was clearly of the highest importance. Modernization was on the way in many countries, but it made all the difference whether the monarch was a Henry II, full of initiative, or an indecisive and weak king like Louis VII, his contemporary on the French throne.[57] Many experiments had been going on for some time in England and Normandy and no essential element of the Common Law was invented in Henry's day, but he decided which elements were finally to be selected and how they were to fit in with the others. He made the whole work like a system.

We should also not forget that this king disposed of the necessary people and resources. England and Normandy were intellectually very alive and full of enterprising people who were in the forefront of European development. This is well known[58] and applies to the legal field as well as to all others. There was, as we have seen, an Anglo-Norman school of canonists: Arnulf of Séez, the first Anglo-Norman clerk to study civil law in Italy of whom we have record, in the early 1130s[59] was followed by many others till the first half of the thirteenth century;[60] a fine example of their international careers can be found in the life of Gervase of Tilbury, the author of the *Otia Imperialia*.[61] The Italian civilian Vacarius came to England in the time of Stephen to teach and do legal business; he wrote a compendium of Roman law, the *Liber Pauperum*, for the poor students who could not afford the whole *Corpus*, and his school – the *pauperistae* – flourished at Oxford in the second half of the twelfth century. English libraries of the time contained a rich selection of books bearing the Bolognese imprint[62] and people made use of them.[63] If England did not receive an exceptional number of papal decretals, it was exception-

100

ally zealous in collecting them in the days of the lawgiver-pope Alexander III, so that in the classical collections of papal decretals an extraordinary proportion concerns English affairs.[64] General education, among laymen too, made great progress[65] and it was possible to recruit for the royal bench a considerable number of justices of oustanding quality. Few had received a formal education in civil or canon law,[h] but many must have had a passing acquaintance with it, since an elementary knowledge was widespread among clerics and ecclesiastical and lay litigation was often in the same hands. These justices, laymen and clerics, became real professionals and without them no Common Law could have developed.[66]

It was not because they knew Roman law or knew of it that Henry II's subjects automatically approved, or wanted to apply it. They were capable of critical judgment and of rejecting Roman law, in spite of their respect for its positive virtues. Sometimes they preferred the customs of their country, particularly as they were applied in the court of their royal master – not every cleric was enthusiastic about the new papal laws either. Thus Ralph Niger in the later years of Henry II's reign defended native law and the judgments of the existing courts against the attacks of the civilians. Roman law, he admitted, had great qualities. It helped, for example, to abolish the *pravus ritus judiciorum*, the bad use of ordeals, which was a good thing. But it was abused by unscrupulous people who twisted the law and tried to break down established customs for their own ends 'enticing the hearts of the men of Israel'. Their attempt at supremacy had been going on in Italy, but lately the creeping wave seeking *regnum et dominatum* had encroached on these western lands and this calamity was spreading through Europe like the revolt of Absalom.[67] Criticism of the new learned law and lawyers, the 'strand of anti-legalism in medieval thought'[68] was by no means an English phenomenon, but was widespread in Europe and particularly in Germany, where the battle-cry 'Juristen, böse Christen'[69] went up against the reception of Roman law. Nevertheless we find it in England at a particularly early date. The defenders of national laws in England did not hesitate to

---

h In France in the thirteenth century the situation was different, many more graduates in law were available to man the Paris Parliament and other courts and make possible the wholesale introduction of Romano-canonical procedure; the rise of the Common Law came too early for this.

produce false papal letters with clear political overtones to bolster their resistance to innovations inspired by Roman law, as is shown by the forgery around 1206–10, probably by a Londoner, of a long letter allegedly from Pope Eleutherius to the British King Lucius. The pope writes: 'the laws of Rome and Caesar we can always reprove, God's law never' and proceeds to forbid King Lucius to use Roman law, and to tell him: 'you should make the law *per consilium regni vestri*'.[70] This was not theoretical talk or theoretical fear. In the early thirteenth century the Sicilian kingdom was being made into a model state where imperial Roman law was the prime mover and not the *consilium regni*, i.e. where the Romanist adage 'conditor et interpres legum solus est imperator' held sway, and not the Germanic and feudal ideas of the necessary consent of the people and of legislation and government by the king with the council of his barons. In England too there were clear 'absolutist' tendencies at work.[71]

Confidence in the customs of the realm and pride in the royal courts that administered them so efficiently[72] were strong dams against the first civilian waves, whose strength at this early stage was not yet comparable to the maturity and prestige of later centuries. The smattering of Roman law found in the English judiciary probably exercised a liberating effect and gave people the intellectual stimulus to turn the pages of the past and to grasp and expound the judicial practice of the triumphant central courts in a systematic way. The Treatise called Glanvill, their greatest achievement, is typical: its substance is in no way Roman, but some Bolognese inspiration is unmistakable. It was not much, but probably just enough to inoculate the royal judiciary against joining 'Absalom's revolt' wholeheartedly and adopting Roman law wholesale.

If Henry II could call on good brains, he also had the wealth to employ them. Ever since Anglo-Saxon times England had been rich,[73] as William the Bastard had not failed to notice. The economic expansion of the twelfth century put considerable new resources at the kings' disposal, which they tapped in a variety of old and new ways, taxing the increasing urban wealth as well as that of the rural landowners. In addition there was a general rise of manorial incomes. Henry II was possibly the wealthiest ruler in Europe, his financial administration was certainly the most efficient and in the best years his income in England must have been about equal to that of the whole English baronage.[74] However, running the kingdom along more modern lines proved very costly. The judicial machinery he set up was on a scale that had never been seen before and those hundreds of royal justices and personnel, touring the country or sitting at Westminster, must have caused considerable expense: not all of it could be covered by employing clerks who could draw on church prebends!

It is true that justice yielded profits.[75] But it is easy to overstress this aspect and to talk loosely of 'the financially profitable' eyres[76] (without calculating what they cost) or even to maintain that profit was the ulterior motive behind Henry II's judicial policy, that 'the preservation of order, the evolution of a common law, the dispensation of justice, were accidentals, the superb consequences of a meaner motive' and to quote the 'fundamental truth of the medieval dictum: *justitia est magnum emolumentum*'.[77] This was not how Henry's contemporary Peter of Blois saw it, when he wrote about the king's great wealth: 'ad pacem populi spectat immensitas illa pecuniarum'.[78] It is not difficult to write about legal reforms in terms of money-seeking, for money did play a rôle in them, as a glance at the pipe rolls shows – but where does it not? There must be few fields of human endeavour where money is completely absent. Shall we quote Beethoven's precise letters on royalties to Breitkopf & Härtel or Peters or Schott & Sons and his concern with the timing of the bills of exchange, and conclude that his symphonies were sophisticated ways of making money?[79] Shall we write the history of Parliament in terms of the chronic demands of members for higher salaries? Or write about medieval monasteries as if they were financial companies with interests in land and money lending? It could be done, but it would miss the point. It does not make sense to suggest that Henry's judicial initiatives were really so many devices to make money.[80] The revenue of the penal operation under the Assize of Clarendon and the repression of unlawful disseisins that went with it has been calculated. In the years 1166–71 the royal revenue from the chattels of those condemned under it (their lands went to their lords) amounted to £312[81] and that from amercements for unlawful disseisins to about £200. We do not know the cost of the eyres, so we cannot compare it with these revenues (also the eyres dealt with other, profitable, business as well), but if we compare these judicial profits with the total English revenue of Henry II calculated at about £35,000 a year,[82] it is at once clear how insignificant they were. And what an elaborate, onerous and far-fetched way of filling the royal chest, when the king could and did use such simple methods as levying huge arbitrary forest fines[83] or leaving some bishopric vacant for a little longer to receive a yearly extra income of over £1,000, without any trouble.[84]

Everybody in the twelfth century knew that you could not obtain justice for nothing, that it had to be paid for like anything else, whether it was at the papal curia or at that of the king. The lower ecclesiastical echelons knew an exaction before trial of two and a half shillings, elegantly called 'the penny of justice'.[1] This was not new. Even before the Normans came the wheels of justice had to be oiled by gifts to the king, without forgetting the queen who expected her percentage,[85] and for many centuries afterwards the parties paid the men who had to judge them, like the students paid the professors who had to examine them and did so, we confidently hope, freely and objectively. Richard fitz Neal, who must have seen some shady bargains at the Exchequer, uses the following lofty words to whitewash them:

'We are, of course, aware that kingdoms are governed and laws maintained primarily by prudence, fortitude, temperance and justice, and the other virtues, for which reason the rulers of the world must practise them with all their might, but there are occasions on which sound and wise schemes take effect earlier through the agency of money, and apparent difficulties are smoothed away by it, as though by skilful negotiation.'[86]

It was in such circumstances that the new Anglo-Norman system of law and procedure was born. Political history explains why it slowly withered away in Normandy and why, after Bannockburn, it was dropped in Scotland (where it had penetrated in the thirteenth century), leaving England alone with her Common Law. In Normandy and Scotland Henry II's creation eventually gave way to the Roman laws that were conquering Europe. Thus, because the Common Law had become part and parcel of her political constitu-

---

[1] Peter the Chanter wonders whether this was simony. He tells us that it was also customary for judges to accept two or three shillings from parties after achieving a settlement. He cites the examiners of witnesses who charge for recording testimonies or even for speeding up their services. Alluding to Roman law and to Augustine's prohibition, the Pope forbade ecclesiastical judges delegate exacting a customary tenth of the suit as security on a salary (Baldwin, *Masters, Princes and Merchants*, I, 191).

tion, an element of her national conscience and the foundation of her social order, England became an island in the Romanist sea. Her semi-feudal, semi-modern Common Law, the most Germanic of Europe, was an anomaly, a freak in the history of western civilization, less modern because it was modernized earlier – a common phenomenon in the history of science and technology.[87] The time factor was of crucial importance.[88] In the rest of Europe legal modernization took place later, under the influence of Roman or Roman inspired doctrine, which had reached scientific maturity and was practised in the Church courts for everyone to see.[89] Because there was a legal void to be filled the kings of England had accomplished a less radical modernization a few generations before Roman law and procedure were ready to offer a fully elaborated model for modernization and before the practical possibilities in terms of university trained personnel were available. Its product however was adequate for the needs of the time and the Common Law, this accident of chronology, continued on its own solitary course.[90]

To a continental observer in the early sixteenth century the Common Law must have looked quaintly antiquated and hopelessly medieval, full of archaic elements, which elsewhere had been swept away like cobwebs by Romanist doctrines: a fossil from the days of western feudalism, of which the Anglo-Normans could hide the fact that it was rooted in antiquated and provincial French law – and 'Norman law was the most feudal of all medieval customs'[91] – just as its technical language was outmoded provincial French. It struck Englishmen travelling on the Continent. Thomas Starkey (†1538), *legum doctor* of an Italian university, possibly Padua, intended on his return to England in 1534, 'to consider and weigh the customs and manners of his countrymen with the policy used here in our nation'. He criticized the law, which he found 'without order or end' and in need of codification in English. All lawyers ought to be instructed in Roman law; indeed the best remedy would be to do away with English law altogether and to 'receyue the cyuyle law of the Romaynys, the wych ys now the commyn law almost of al Chrystyan natyonys'. He was particularly indignant at 'the grete schame to our natyon the grete infamy and rote that remeynyth in vs, to be gouernyd by the lawys gyuen to vs of such a barbarouse natyon as the Normannys be'.[92] Nothing came of his sweeping plans and English law, the first to modernize, was

105

the last to remove certain procedural archaisms.[93] Some of the Common Law's obvious imperfections were remedied from the late Middle Ages onwards by the Equity jurisdiction of the Court of Chancery, whose outlook was strongly Romano-canonical – a price paid for the precocious nature of the Common Law. The sixteenth century witnessed the growing importance of the prerogative courts and even some attempts by Henry VIII to introduce Roman law, but the seventeenth century saw the triumph of the Common Law, which conserved its essential procedure until the great reforms of the nineteenth and much of its substantive law until our day.

Readers who like some philosophy with their history will find food for reflection here. The rôle of the Common Law has been enduring and immense in many countries on several continents. Yet the capital period of its foundation was very brief: in less than two generations, say between the assize of novel disseisin and the loss of Normandy, the crucial decisions were taken that would eventually lead to the rise of the 'Anglo-Saxon legal family', one of the four or five systems of truly universal significance. Also, it is impossible not to be struck by the rôle of sheer coincidence in the birth of this European anomaly. 'Chance' or 'coincidence' is a difficult philosophical concept, which the historian uses at his peril, but that should not stop him using it, if he believes that it can help the understanding of historical events. So, when we speak of the chance element in the birth of the Common Law, we should be aware that we are in rather treacherous waters. We should also realize that we deal with something fundamental in historical research. Many historians felt that, if the *explanation* of the past is what history is about, we ought to look for laws and recurrences,[94] the determinism of certain great factors, the underlying mass movements and the like. We ought to steer clear of chance or historical accident as the great spoil-sport. If history is to be taken as a serious art-form endowed with universality – and thus to escape the strictures of Aristotle – we must group and explain events so that their apparent chaos becomes an organized system presenting a coherent picture, ordered and comprehended by our intelligence, however disconnected in fact events may be.[95]

In this perspective, chance, the great irrational factor, is the skeleton in the cupboard, hushed up and kept out of sight as a disreputable interloper, which, if it is occasionally mentioned, gets

106

very short shrift indeed. To attribute important historical developments, for example the origin of modern science, entirely to chance
is, we read, 'to declare the bankruptcy of history as a form of
enlightenment of the human mind'.[96] But why should everything in
history be explicable in terms of laws and logic? Could it be to
give us a sense of certainty and domination over events of the past –
even if we cannot control them at present – and of superiority over
the 'mere empirical investigator with his collections of data and
his tentative approximations'?[97] Some historians clearly feel that
the invocation of the chance factor is a clear sign of decadence in
a scholar. Thus we read that Pirenne in his 'great years', mainly
thanks to the influence of Lamprecht, had determinist views and,
in a Hegelian vein, believed that history could be explained in terms
of regularities and recurrencies; also that he believed in the decisive
rôle of the 'anonymous forces' and mass-movements essentially of
an economic character and felt close to historical materialism,
writing 'the two first volumes of the *Histoire de Belgique* as if he
were won over to historical materialism'. It is true that towards the
end of his life he thought differently and lectured on the importance
of chance in history; 'this fact, we are told, was invoked to deny
that he believed in determinism, yet that is to forget that human
intelligence develops, and not necessarily towards greater per-
fection'.[98] Nevertheless, emboldened by support from an unexpected
quarter – I mean the essay on the rôle of chance in the origin and
development of the biosphere by the eminent biochemist J. Monod[99]
– I feel that the rôle of chance in history in general and in the
establishment of the Common Law in particular has been too
striking to be passed in silence.

To begin with, the exceptional strength of the English monarchy
in the crucial years was the result of two phenomena that had no
inner relationship, the rise of a unified state in Anglo-Saxon times,
and its conquest by the Normans. While the Franks were paying the
penalty of disintegration for overreaching themselves in the pursuit
of 'Old Empires and their ghosts', the English kings successfully
limited themselves to the consolidation of national unity; that their
country was eventually occupied by a powerful line of feudal con-
querors resulted from an altogether different train of events, but
it gave additional power to the central government and signified that
English kings – feudal overlords could easily become the focus for
all free tenants and their court develop a law common to them. This

exceptional strength put England a couple of generations ahead in the race for developed political institutions and the establishment of a modernized system of law and courts. It effectively excluded Roman law which had not yet reached sufficient maturity to be a serious competitor. However, there is no causal connection between the timing of the Bolognese success and that of the English royal courts. What feudal kings were doing in England was immaterial to the glossators and canonists in northern Italy, the timing of their teaching and its European diffusion had no causal connection with the developments in England – except in the vaguest sense of a general European progress of civilization. That Roman and canon law reached maturity and European application just after the Common Law was established, can only be called a matter of chronological chance, a coincidence. In the same way it was a coincidence that Roman and canon law were readily at hand when Louis IX decided to modernize French courts, and that they had completed their medieval career by the time the Germans 'received' them in their turn.[100] The schools, the Roman *curia* and the officialities did not time their progress according to the internal policies of the European kingdoms.

Their timing had even less connection with various fortuitous circumstances on the English scene, such as the accession to the throne, about two generations before the learned law reached a position of strength, of a ruler with the interest and the ambition to modernize justice – not a universal trait of kings. And it was a coincidence again that Henry II ruled after Stephen and Matilda had created such chaos that the country was ripe for the stern, nation-wide clean-up of the Assizes and the liquidation of judicial contradictions and uncertainties through centralization in the royal courts[101] – a notable factor in hastening the reform movement at a moment when time was important. Whether Roman law would provide the substance for the modernized law of the late medieval semi-bureaucratic state or only a limited contribution, sufficient to give an intellectual stimulus to a native development, was very much a question of timing.

The importance of timing can be seen all along in the historical difference between England and the Continent. Their development was so divergent not because the basic elements of English civilization were different – we share them all, the mediterranean and the Germanic traditions, Christianity in its catholic and protestant forms, urban life, the monarchy and parliaments, the universities and science, the arts and agriculture, trade and industry – but because the timing of their appearance and influence was different. The ingredients are the same, the rhythm of their impact, the succession of their ups and downs was different. This was true from the start and is most striking if one makes the comparison with the nearest big country on the Continent, Gaul or France. In the eighth century civilization in Gaul and the Frankish Church had reached rock-bottom, while the England of Bede, Boniface and Alcuin was a beacon in the night and saved the kingdom of the Franks by a massive assistance programme. When the Continent became feudal in the Carolingian and post-Carolingian era, England did not share this development. Not until after 1066 did feudalism reach her shores, on the eve, ironically, of the European decline of feudalism as a political and military force. In the twelfth century the English state was the most advanced model, imitated by the Capetians. Feudalism in England has not been allowed to realize its disruptive potentiality and even strengthened royal power; but when Angevin kingship began to overstep the boundaries, when royal *vis et voluntas* and even *ira et malevolentia* were becoming intolerable and the personal rule of the monarchy undermined the rule of law, feudalism supplied the constitutional framework for resistance. The revolting barons took their stand on feudal law and followed its formalities. For, if the king was their divinely ordained ruler he was also their feudal lord and as such had obligations towards them; king and barons had entered into a contract and the contractual nature of medieval feudalism coloured the whole constitutional outlook of the period.[102] Thus England ignored feudalism when it could have undermined the state, but had it ready at hand, when it served, without endangering the integrity of the state, to check royal power.[103] This seems to be feudalism at its best and it is one of the paradoxes of history that kings and lords of French extraction built in England a better feudal system than at home: this feudal law, the stone which the continental builders disallowed, when they turned to Roman law, became the cornerstone of the Common Law.[j] It played a great and rather unexpected rôle in the seventeenth century. When royal absolutism triumphed on the

---

[j] It is ironic that the adoption in England eight centuries ago of a system of continental origin, that was subsequently given up in its land of origin, should now be a major obstacle to European legal unification.

109

Continent, the English Parliament stood its ground and overcame the monarchy, the deplorable triumph – so it seemed to many – of a medieval relic over modern, progressive forms of government.[104] The Common Law and the powerful lobby of the common lawyers in Parliament were instrumental in this victory,[105] and we have here the amazing spectacle of a legal system inaugurated by French kings and a French feudal aristocracy in the twelfth century buttressing the English Parliament in the seventeenth.[106] But what is backward and scorned in one century is modern and craved for in the next: the eighteenth and nineteenth centuries greatly admired England's institutions; her Gothic parliament, however medieval in origin and structure, became the dream of liberal revolutionaries and the keystone of modern civilized states on the Continent.

No doubt more illustrations of this long *chassé-croisé* could be found, and the use of the Common Law is only one episode among others, but we must conclude. Who was out of step with whom, England with the Continent or vice versa? The answer will depend on the point of view, just as to the question whether in case of fog over the Channel Britain is cut off from the Continent or the Continent from Britain. I shall not venture to give my own answer,[107] but will only submit the paradox that the Common Law, which became a real hallmark of English life, was originally not English at all. It was a species of continental feudal law developed into an English system by kings and justices of continental extraction. Within a few generations, this exotic innovation took on the protective colouring of a thoroughly native species,[108] but to see through this veil and to point out the true provenance and real origin of the Common Law is the historian's duty.

Notes to the Text

CHAPTER 1 PAGES 1–28

1 See, for example, the *Leges Henrici Primi*, a private compilation from the middle of Henry I's reign, ed. F. Liebermann, *Die Gesetze der Angelsachsen*, I (Halle, 1903), 547–611. For a recent assessment, see H. G. Richardson and G. O. Sayles, *Law and Legislation from Æthelberht to Magna Carta* (Edinburgh, 1966), pp. 43–5.

2 See the lists in R. V. Turner, *The King and His Courts. The role of John and Henry III in the administration of justice, 1199–1240* (Ithaca, N.Y., 1968), pp. 280–5.

3 A most useful collection of miscellaneous texts throwing light on legal procedure was published by the American lawyer M. M. Bigelow under the title *Placita Anglo-Normannica. Law cases from William I to Richard I* (Boston, 1879). The editor, however, did not use manuscript material and many of his texts are, of course, now available in better editions than the ones at his disposal.

4 W. Ullmann, *The Individual and Society in the Middle Ages* (Baltimore, 1966 and London, 1967), p. 96.

5 C. Johnson, *The Course of the Exchequer by Richard, son of Nigel*, Medieval Classics (London, 1950), p. 53.

6 C. W. Hollister, *Anglo-Saxon Military Institutions* (Oxford, 1962) and *The Military Organization of Norman England* (Oxford, 1965).

7 F. L. Ganshof, *Feudalism*, trans. Ph. Grierson (3rd Eng. ed., London, 1964), p. 165. See on the absence of feudalism in pre-Conquest England: R. A. Brown, 'The Norman Conquest', *Transactions of the Royal Historical Society*, 5th ser., 17 (1967), 120–7.

8 F. Barlow, *The Feudal Kingdom of England* (London, 1963), p. 437.

9 H. G. Richardson and G. O. Sayles, *The Governance of mediaeval England from the Conquest to Magna Carta* (Edinburgh, 1963), pp. 27, 33 and 118.

10 See M. W. Bean, *The Decline of English Feudalism 1215–1540* (Manchester and New York, 1968) and J. J. N. Palmer, 'The last summons of the feudal army in England (1385)', *Eng. Hist. Rev.*, 83 (1968), 771–6.

11 Thus H. Parker, *Observations upon some of his Majesties late Answers and Expresses* (1642), p. 3, quoted in C. Hill, *Puritanism and Revolution. Studies in Interpretations of the English Revolution of the 17th Century* (London, 1958), p. 77.

12 Quoted in H. M. Cam, *Law-Finders and Law-Makers in medieval England. Collected studies in legal and constitutional history* (London, 1962), p. 224. F. M. Stenton, *The first century of English feudalism* (2nd edn., Oxford, 1961) remains the classic work. On the 'Round–Freeman controversy' we mention further the following most recent studies: E. John, 'English Feudalism and the Structure of Anglo-Saxon Society', *Bulletin of the John Rylands Library*, 46 (1963–4), 14–41 (repr. in his *Orbis Britanniae and other Studies*, Leicester, 1966, pp. 128–53) [an extreme exposition of the 'continuity' thesis]; 'Two Comments on the Problem of Continuity in Anglo-Norman Feudalism', I by C. W. Hollister, II by J. C. Holt, *Economic History Review*, 2nd ser., 16 (1963–4),

104–13, 114–18, and C. W. Hollister, '1066. The "feudal revolution"',
American Historical Review, 73 (1967–8), 708–23; J. Beeler, 'The composition of Anglo-Norman armies, *Speculum*, 40 (1965), 398–414 [all
against the continuity thesis]; R. A. Brown, 'The Norman Conquest',
pp. 109–30, contains a demonstration of the absence of feudalism in
Anglo-Saxon society and state; in the same sense: D. C. Douglas,
William the Conqueror. The Norman impact upon England (London
1964), pp. 265–88.

13 Cam, *Law-Finders*, p. 58.

14 D. Knowles, 'Archbishop Thomas Becket: a Character Study', *Proceedings of the British Academy*, 35 (1949) (= *The Historian and
Character* (Cambridge, 1963), p. 101).

15 Douglas, *William the Conqueror*, pp. 60 and 379.

16 F. Pollock and F. W. Maitland, *The History of English Law before the
time of Edward I* (2nd edn, Cambridge, 1898), ɪɪ p. 459.

17 See *Studi Medievali*, 3rd ser., 6 (1965), 307–8.

18 For a recent critical look, see P. Chaplais, 'The Anglo-Saxon Chancery:
from the diploma to the writ', *Journal of the Society of Archivists*, 3
(1966), 160–76. The author maintains that all the royal diplomas of
Edward the Confessor (and his predecessors) and even some of his
writs were written in ecclesiastical scriptoria for, or by, the recipients,
so that the chancery inherited by the Conqueror, who had had neither
a seal nor a chancery at home, was not as highly developed as has
been imagined. Nevertheless the uniformity of many surviving writs
clearly points to a well organized and permanent royal writing-office in
England before the Conquest, which was maintained and developed by
the Conqueror. Not much more was needed or could be expected than
a seal, an official to look after it and a few royal scribes who wrote the
king's correspondence and administrative orders, to speak of a chancery, or writing-office or royal secretariat (after all, the Carolingian
chancery worked with a chancellor and on average about three *notarii*).
See also the tentative remarks in F. Barlow, *The English Church 1000–
1066. A Constitutional History* (London, 1963), pp. 120–28: no 'proper
writing-office' but a 'formless secretariat'; and, of course, the fundamental pages in F. E. Harmer, *Anglo-Saxon Writs* (Manchester, 1952),
pp. 57–61.

19 H. M. Cam, 'The Evolution of the mediaeval English franchise',
Speculum, 32 (1957), 427–42.

20 Barlow, *The English Church*, p. 300. See also H. R. Loyn, 'The King
and the structure of Society in Late Anglo-Saxon England', *History*, 42
(1957), 87–100.

21 J.-F. Lemarignier, *Le gouvernement royal aux premiers temps capétiens*
(Paris, 1965), pp. 159–63.

22 M. Prou, *Recueil des actes de Philippe Ier roi de France* (Paris, 1908),
nr 84, p. 220; cf. K. F. Werner, 'Königtum und Fürstentum im französischen 12. Jahrhundert', *Probleme des 12. Jahrhunderts, Vorträge
und Forschungen*, 12 (Konstanz/Stuttgart, 1968), 179. See also W.
Kienast, 'Der Wirkungsbereich des französischen Königtums von Odo
bis Ludwig VI (888–1137) in Südfrankreich', *Historische Zeitschrift*, 209
(1970), 529–65.

23 See F. Barlow, *Edward the Confessor* (London, 1970), p. 186. The
author does not suppose there was anything 'very elaborate' but believes that the royal treasury was 'something rather more sophisticated

than was usual in eleventh-century Europe'; see also B. Lyon and A. Verhulst, *Medieval Finance. A Comparison of Financial Institutions in North-western Europe*, Rijksuniversiteit Gent. Werken Fac. Letteren, 143 (Bruges, 1967), pp. 56–60.

24 Richardson and Sayles, *Law and Legislation*, p. 30.

25 Richardson and Sayles, *Governance*, p. 27.

26 See J. Boussard, 'La notion de royauté sous Guillaume le Conquérant. Ses origines et ses prolongements', *Annali della Fondazione Italiana per la Storia Amministrativa*, 4 (1967), 47–77.

27 F. W. Maitland, *Domesday Book and Beyond* (Cambridge, 1897), p. 103.

28 C. Morris, 'William I and the church courts', *Eng. Hist. Rev.*, 82 (1967), 449–63: the shire-courts continued to deal with ecclesiastical affairs for a long time and a fully established network of Church courts with their own personnel and procedure took a long time to arise. The text is in W. Stubbs, *Select Charters* (9th edn, Oxford, 1913), pp. 99–100.

29 Richardson and Sayles, *Governance*, pp. 156–66 open the 'Age of the Justiciars' with Roger le Poer, bishop of Salisbury, being appointed chief justiciar in 1109 and link the institution of the office with the conquest of Normandy (1106) and the consequent absenteeism of English kings on the Continent. F. West, *The Justiciarship in England 1066–1232* (Cambridge, 1966), though admitting (p. 18) that Roger's 'position certainly bore two strong resemblances to the justiciarship', feels that the office does not clearly and finally emerge before Henry II's time, with the justiciarship held by two men, Earl Robert of Leicester and Richard de Lucy. The official disappeared before the middle of the thirteenth century, his 'viceregal raison d'être' was gone with the loss of Normandy in 1204.

30 Thus the jaundiced remark of Orderic Vitalis, ed. A. Le Prévost (5 vols. Paris, 1838–55), IV, 164.

31 H. A. Cronne, 'The Office of Local Justiciar in England under the Norman Kings', *University of Birmingham Historical Journal*, 6 (1957), 18–38 traces the office of shire justiciar further back than Henry I, but the evidence is scanty; cf. Richardson and Sayles, *Governance*, pp. 173–4, 194–5. D. M. Stenton, *English Justice between the Norman Conquest and the Great Charter 1066–1215*, Jayne Lectures for 1963 (Philadelphia, 1964), pp. 65–8 underlines the necessity of 'breaking down the con-centration of functions – executive, judicial, financial and military – which was turning the shire reeve of King Æthelræd's time into an officer of state more powerful than any but the greatest of Æthelræd's earls', hence 'the removal of the pleas of the crown from the jurisdiction of the Sheriff, and the creation of a local justiciar in each shire or recognised group of shires, with the specific duty of hearing them', and maintains that although the court of the local justiciar may have met where the shire court met, it was not the shire court'; cf. H. A. Cronne, *The Reign of Stephen 1135–54. Anarchy in England* (London, 1970), pp. 257–9.

32. S. Painter, *Studies in the history of the English feudal barony*, The Johns Hopkins University Studies in Historical and Political Science, LXI, 3 (Baltimore, 1943), 111–12: 'But in respect to pleas commenced by these new writs [of the Common Law] the sheriff was merely an errand boy'. The use of this term has been criticized by historians who felt that the office of sheriff was underestimated. It is, however, a good description of the sheriff's rôle as far as the performance of various

tasks in connection with the Common Law writs, such as summoning
parties and juries, returning writs, giving seisin in execution of judgments is concerned. Professor Milsom puts it, more diplomatically, as
follows: 'From presiding over what was, for all ordinary purposes, the
most important kind of court in the land, he slowly became the executive addressee of commands from higher central bodies' (S. F. C. Milsom, *Historical Foundations of the Common Law* (London, 1969), p. 4).

33 C. 31, 7, ed. Liebermann, *Gesetze der Angelsachsen*, I, 564.
34 Stubbs, *Select Charters*, p. 122; *Regesta Regum Anglo-Normannorum*,
II, nr 892, p. 82, dated [1108, May–July].
35 C. 25, 2, ed. Liebermann, *Gesetze*, I, 562.
36 C. 7, 1–7, 3, *ibid.*, p. 553: 'Intersint autem episcopi, comites, vice-
domini . . . Agantur itaque primo debita vere christianitatis iura; secundo
regis placita, postremo cause singulorum dignis satisfaccionibus
expleantur' – the text corresponds with Cnut's Law, 18 and 18, 1 (*ibid.*,
p. 320), but is far from a literal copy and much more elaborate.
37 While a bishop surrounded by his *curia episcopalis* might hold pleas
as a prelate on spiritual matters, he could also hold pleas on feudal
matters, surrounded by his vassals as in any other baronial *curia*, and
the distinction is not always easy to make.
38 Constitutions of Clarendon, 1164, c. 9, ed. Stubbs, *Select Charters*, pp.
165–6.
39 C. 1, *ibid.*, p. 164; see Richardson and Sayles, *Governance*, pp. 314–16.
40 R. C. van Caenegem, *Royal Writs in England from the Conquest to
Glanvill. Studies in the Early History of the Common Law*, Selden Soc.
vol. 77 (London, 1959), pp. 25 and 41ff.
41 N. D. Hurnard, *The King's Pardon for Homicide before A.D. 1307*
(Oxford, 1969), pp. viii–ix; cf. our remarks in *Studi Medievali*, ser. 3,
11 (1970), 996–7.
42 Liebermann, *Gesetze*, I, 552–3.
43 Richardson and Sayles, *Law and Legislation*, p. 96.
44 *Ibid.*, p. 98.
45 Cronne, *Stephen*, p. 253.
46 John of Salisbury, quoted in Turner, *The King and His Courts*, p. 185.
47 C. 6, 2, ed. Liebermann, *Gesetze*, I, 552.
48 Johnson, *Course of the Exchequer*, p. 1. Richard, the author of the
Dialogue, was the son of Nigel, bishop of Ely, treasurer of Henry I and
nephew of the powerful Roger of Salisbury.
49 *Ibid.*
50 See the chapter (III) of that title in J. E. A. Jolliffe, *Angevin Kingship*
(2nd edn, London, 1963), pp. 50–86.
51 D. M. Stenton, *English Society in the Early Middle Ages (1066–1307)*
(2nd edn, Harmondsworth, 1952), p. 162: 'At Christmas 1125 the
moneyers were summoned to Winchester and there they were taken one
by one and deprived of their right hands and emasculated. The Anglo-
Saxon Chronicle says that this dour business was completed by Twelfth
Night'; see the remarks of Richardson and Sayles, *Law and Legislation*,
p. 34.
52 A. L. Poole, *From Domesday Book to Magna Carta 1087–1216*, Oxford
History of England (Oxford, 1951), p. 389: the majority of the old
sheriffs were dismissed and replaced by men who were already em-
ployed at the Exchequer, professional administrators rather than
influential magnates.

53 See, for example, a writ of Henry II (*anno* 1157?) to Cecily de Muschamp and Thomas, her son, which runs as follows: 'Miror et displicet
mihi multum quod . . . non fecistis quod vobis precepi per alia brevia
mea. Nunc autem precipio firmiter . . .', ed. Van Caenegem, *Writs*, p.
435, nr 47*a*. Cf. the *contradictio precepti mei* in M. Gibbs, *Early charters of the cathedral church of St. Paul*, Camden Soc., 3rd ser., vol. 58
(London, 1939), nr 24, p. 21 – *Regesta Regum Anglo-Normannorum*,
II, nr 605, p. 25, A.D. 1101–2.
54 Pollock and Maitland, *History of English Law*, II, 666–8.
55 See a writ of Henry I of Easter 1101 to Osbert, sheriff, and Richard son
of Gotse, directing *inter alia* that Gerard, archbishop of York, shall
pursue in his own court offences against 'my new statutes concerning
the trial of thieves and false moneyers' and that he 'shall lose no judicial
income because of my new statutes, but, as I said, he shall apply them
in his own court by his own justice, according to my statutes', ed. W.
Farrer, *Early Yorkshire Charters*, I (Edinburgh, 1914), nr 14, p. 31,
Regesta Regum Anglo-Normannorum, II, nr 518, pp. 7–8; cf. Richardson and Sayles, *Law and Legislation*, p. 34.
56 That the *curia regis* and the *curia regis ad scaccarium* were not the
same thing, is clear from an entry in Pipe Roll 34 Henry II, p. 155,
where we find Ricardus filius Meini owing 3 marks to have his case
in curia regis and another mark to have the same case (*eadem loquela*)
'in curia regis apud scaccarium'.
57 Richardson and Sayles, *Governance*, p. 175.
58 See the note on 'The Eyre of 1166' in J. C. Holt, 'The Assizes of
Henry II: the Texts', *The Study of Medieval Records. Essays in honour
of Kathleen Major*, ed. by D. A. Bullough and R. L. Storey (Oxford,
1971), pp. 101–6. Even in the counties which the justices did not visit
the Assize of Clarendon was applied, presumably by the sheriffs and the
local justices.
59 Turner, *The King and His Courts*, pp. 34ff.
60 See R. W. Eyton, *Court, household, and itinerary of King Henry II*
(Cornhill, 1878); H. G. Richardson, 'Richard fitz Neal and the
Dialogus de Scaccario', *Eng. Hist. Rev.* 43 (1928), 167–71; J. Boussard,
Le Gouvernement d'Henri II Plantagenêt (Paris, 1956), pp. 494–518 and
passim; Van Caenegem, *Writs*, pp. 16–34; Richardson and Sayles,
Governance, pp. 173–215; Stenton, *English Justice*, pp. 54–87; W. T.
Reedy, 'The origins of the general eyre in the reign of Henry I',
Speculum, 41 (1966), 688–724; Richardson and Sayles, *Law and Legisla-
tion*, pp. 88–90 and *passim*; D. M. Stenton, *Pleas before the King or
his Justices 1198–1212*, III, Selden Soc., vol. 83 (London, 1967),
xlvii–ccxciv (fundamental); Turner, *The King and His Courts*; Milsom,
Historical Foundations, pp. 16–22.
61 I consulted with profit K. J. Stringer's unpublished dissertation, 'The
General Eyres in the Reign of Henry II' (Newcastle, s.d.), which
the author put at my disposal in 1968, for which many thanks. On the
standard of learning, see the interesting pages in Richardson and
Sayles, *Governance*, pp. 265–84.
62 Stenton, *English Justice*, p. 84 draws attention to 'laymen of undistin-
guished origin . . . generally the first of their families to rise from
rustic obscurity. Sometimes they are the younger sons of modestly
landed families . . . One eminent judge of the next generation was certainly of English descent . . . But nothing is known of the origin of the

115

Wiltshire James of Potterne, the Sussex John of Guestling, the Hampshire Richard of Herriard.' C. R. Cheney, *From Becket to Langton. English Church Government 1170–1213*, The Ford Lectures 1955 (Manchester, 1956), p. 24 points out that in the period under review seventeen bishops combined the duties of bishop and royal judge.

63 Glanvill, xii, 25, ed. Hall, p. 148. The writ of right, as Hall remarks, had in it the threat of removal to the county court. Thus, in effect if not in intent, the rule assisted the flow of cases from feudal to royal courts; cf. Glanvill, xii, 2, p. 137. In xii, 25 Glanvill specifically mentions the court of a lord. In xii, 2 he makes no such restriction and says quite generally that 'when anyone claims to hold of another by free service any free tenement or service, he may not implead *the tenant* about it without a writ from the lord king or his justices' – application to feudal courts was presumably the most frequent.

64 Glanvill, xii, 3, p. 137.

65 This first step cost half a mark. See the text in P. M. Barnes, 'The Anstey Case', *A Medieval Miscellany for Doris Mary Stenton*, ed. P. M. Barnes and C. F. Slade, Pipe Roll Soc., lxxvi (London, 1962), 17–23. On the exact nature of this initial writ see the remarks of Miss Barnes, *ibid.*, pp. 3–4.

66 Painter, *English feudal barony*, p. 39.

67 Canonists and civilists carried on a lively discussion on the number of acts required to establish a custom or to make it manifest, see Le Bras, Lefebvre and Rambaud. *L'âge classique*, pp. 542–50, and the classical work of S. Brie, *Die Lehre vom Gewohnheitsrecht. Eine historisch-dogmatische Untersuchung*, i: *Geschichtliche Grundlegung* (Breslau, 1899), 104ff., 134ff.

68 Stenton, *English Justice*, pp. 27–30.

69 See, for example, Edward Grim's Life of Becket, c. 56, ed. J. C. Robertson, *Materials for the History of Thomas Becket*, Rolls Series, ii (London, 1876), 406: 'Clamatum est ex ore regis quod si quis pro quocumque negotio sedem apostolicam appellasset, omnia quae illius essent scriberentur ad opus regis, et ipse truderetur in carcerem.' The Frankish capitularies had been similarly based on an oral promulgation (F. L. Ganshof, *Was waren die Kapitularien?* (Weimar, 1961), pp. 36–40).

70 Glanvill, xii, 25, p. 148: 'secundum consuetudinem regni'.

71 The defendant's option of choosing trial by jury, based on the Assize of Windsor, is clearly identified as being of legislative origin: 'this assize is a royal benefit granted to the people by the goodness of the king acting on the advice of his magnates, ii, 7, p. 28.

72 Amongst the deperdita in Miss Harmer's *Anglo-Saxon Writs*, we find one by Æthelred II of 990–2, which she translates as follows: 'Then the king sent his seal to the meeting at Cuckamsley by Abbot Ælfhere and greeted all the witan who were assembled there, namely Bishop Æthelsige and Bishop Æscwig and Abbot Ælfric and the whole shire, and prayed and commanded them to settle the case between Wynflæd and Leofwine as justly as they could' (p. 541, Appendix iv, nr 1). It is not certain that there was a writ involved; a spoken message, supported by a royal seal was equally possible. There is no doubt that a writ was used in the case of Snodland in the time of Æthelred II. The king sent his *gewrit and his insegel* to the archbishop of Canterbury directing that he and his thegns in East Kent should settle a disputed claim of the bishop of Rochester (A.D. *c.* 995). On this early example of

a royal writ directing the course of proceedings in a court of law see Harmer, *Anglo-Saxon Writs*, pp. 46–7 and Stenton, *English Justice*, pp. 8–10. We also draw attention to an English writ of Queen Edith, the Confessor's widow, addressed to the hundred of Wedmore, informing it of a grant to the canons of Wells (the reason why it was preserved), but asking also 'that you will pronounce for me a just judgment concerning Wudumann to whom I entrusted my horse(s) and who has for six years withheld my rent', ed. Harmer, *Writs*, nr 72, pp. 285–6, 6 Jan. 1066–19 Dec. 1075, cf. D. Whitelock, 'The Anglo-Saxon Achievement', *The Norman Conquest* (London, 1966), p. 30; there is every reason to believe that other Anglo-Saxon writs to hundred courts have existed, but they were ephemeral documents, not title-deeds and there was therefore not much reason to conserve them if they merely contained an exhortation to a law court.

73 Painter, *English feudal barony*, pp. 170–3.
74 A. L. Poole, *Obligations of Society in the XII and XIII centuries*, The Ford Lectures 1944 (Oxford, 1946), p. 77. See *ibid.*, pp. 77–9 for a discussion of 'the relative value of money' in the twelfth and thirteenth centuries.
75 See on all this Van Caenegem, *Writs*, pp. 212–34.

CHAPTER 2   PAGES 29–61

1 *Curia Regis Rolls*, II (London, 1925), 217, 237, 280, cf. E. De Haas and G. D. G. Hall, *Early Registers of Writs*, Selden Soc., vol. 87 (London, 1970), p. xi.
2 See H. Peter, *Actio und Writ. Eine vergleichende Darstellung römischer und englischer Rechtsbehelfe*, Untersuchungen zur vergleichenden allgemeinen Rechtslehre und zur Methodik der Rechtsvergleichung, vol. 2 (Tübingen, 1957).
3 T. F. T. Plucknett, *A Concise History of the Common Law*, 5th edn (London, 1956), p. 164: 'The issue of a writ from the Chancery was no guarantee that the writ was valid at common law, for the judges asserted their right to quash writs which they considered unsuitable.'
4 See the classic study of F. W. Maitland, 'History of the register of original writs', *Harvard Law Review*, 3 (1889), 97–115 (= *Collected Papers*, II (Cambridge, 1911), 110–73). The so-called Irish Register of 1227 is but nine pages long, with fifty-six entries. In the printed *Registrum Brevium* of 1531 there are 321 folios of original and 85 folios of judicial writs. Original writs were the core of the Register, which therefore is sometimes called Register of Original Writs. See the authoritative edition and commentary in de Haas and Hall, *Early Registers of Writs*. As well as containing the usual collection of original writs, the printed 'Register of Original Writs' also has judicial writs in its latter part and even a considerable number of documents of a miscellaneous character, see P. H. Winfield, *The chief sources of English legal history* (Cambridge, Mass., 1925), p. 301.
5 De Haas and Hall, *op. cit.*, pp. cxvi–cxxiii.
6 *Ibid.*, p. cxxi.
7 Van Caenegem, *Writs*, pp. 113–20.
8 Harmer, *Writs*, nr 33, p. 186; nr 55, pp. 244–5 (A.D. 1053–7); nr 96, pp. 360–1 (A.D. 1065–6); nr 115, pp. 410–11 (A.D. 1062) and possibly nr 11, p. 156 (A.D. 1044–65).

NOTES TO PAGES 31-6

9 See the remarks of G. Barraclough, 'The Anglo-Saxon Writ', *History*, New Series, 39 (1954), p. 206 and V. H. Galbraith, *Studies in the public records* (London, 1948), pp. 35ff.
10 Harmer, *Writs*, pp. 10–13.
11 Chaplais, 'The Anglo-Saxon Chancery', pp. 167–70. The author is surely right in claiming that mention of a seal being sent does not mean – as Miss Harmer thought – that a written (sealed) text was sent as well.
12 *Ibid.*, p. 170; see also pp. 166–7, his remarks on the decline of the diploma and the corresponding (?) rise of the writ.
13 *Ibid.*, pp. 171–2; we have seen this text in the previous chapter, p. 27, n. 72, together with a writ of Queen Edith ordering that 'a just judgement concerning Wudumann be pronounced' for her, Harmer, *Writs*, nr 72, pp. 285–6.
14 Van Caenegem, *Writs*, pp. 113–20.
15 Harmer, *Writs*, pp. 32, 93; Lemarignier, *Gouvernement royal*, pp. 159–62.
16 'Ubi rex ibi lex', reported by Peter the Chanter, see J. W. Baldwin, 'Critics of the legal profession: Peter the Chanter and his Circle', *Proceedings of the Second International Congress of Medieval Canon Law*, Boston, 1963 (Vatican, 1965), p. 250 (Monumenta Iuris Canonici Series C: Subsidia, 1). Peter the Chanter adds: 'ergo canones et iura humana nil habent vigoris'.
17 *Chronicon de Abingdon*, ed. J. Stevenson, Rolls Series, II (London, 1858), 184 explains how Henry II ordered the sheriff to take certain measures against the abbey along purely executive lines in the words 'praecepit ut, ablato omni dilationis scrupulo, causam utramque secundum jus regium tractaret'. Later generations would call this the royal prerogative.
18 R. W. Southern, *Western Society and the Church in the Middle Ages*, The Pelican History of the Church, II (Harmondsworth, 1970), 109.
19 *Ibid.*, p. 110.
20 There is a graphic description of a violent disseisin in a letter of Pope Alexander III of 1159–81. The Cistercian Abbey of Wardon had been the victim of wrongdoers who 'domos illorum violenter infringunt, monacos, conversos, familiares et servientes eorum duris verberibus et conviciis afficiunt, animalia eorum rapiunt, annonam de grangiis illorum et alia bona distrahunt, ferramenta et carrucas eorum in campis furtive subtrahunt, segetes et alia huiusmodi vi, fraude et furto sepius auferre presumunt...' (W. Holtzmann, *Papsturkunden in England*, III (Göttingen, 1952), nr 308, pp. 426–7. Religious houses could, of course, turn to the pope as well as to the king and Holtzmann's volumes of *Papsturkunden* contain numerous papal restitution orders for English houses, with or without judicial procedure.
21 See examples of executive writs, particularly concerning seisin, in Van Caenegem, *Writs*, pp. 189ff. and 267ff. The writ of naifty is a striking example of a fossilized executive writ in the Common Law (Glanvill, XII, 11), see further pp. 55–6.
22 Ed. Stevenson, pp. 183ff., Bigelow, *Placita*, pp. 167ff.; see the comments in Cronne, *Stephen*, pp. 261–2.
23 Cronne, *Stephen*, p. 248.
24 Jolliffe, *Angevin Kingship*, p. 40.
25 See the case of Roger of Luvetot who had lied to the king about the land of Broughton, which was later confirmed to Ramsey Abbey and all

dispute stopped (W. D. Macray, *Chronicon abbatiae Rameseiensis*, Rolls Series (London, 1886), nr 236, p. 232.

26 See the case of one William of Wood who obtained from King John a confirmation of his right to build a windmill at Monkton in Kent to the disadvantage of the priory of Holy Trinity in Canterbury. William had obtained this confirmation by keeping silent about a previous suit on the question and the final concord made in the court of Richard I. When all this was pointed out, the court *coram rege* in 1204 recognized that William had deceived the king and decided that the charter should be annulled and the windmill destroyed, see Turner, *The King and His Courts*, pp. 241-2.

27 In a writ of 1144-52 King Stephen declared that he had given the church of Wolverhampton, which in fact belonged to the prior and monks of the Cathedral of Worcester, to Bishop Roger of Chester 'inconsulte'. After learning about the true situation, he revoked his error and confirmed the monks of Worcester: they were not to be disturbed 'for any writ which the bishop of Chester might produce'! (*Regesta Regum Anglo-Normannorum*, III, nr 969, p. 359; R. R. Darlington, *The Cartulary of Worcester Cathedral Priory (Register I)*, Pipe Roll Soc., 76 (London, 1968), nr 263, p. 139, with the date '1148-53'). People readily suggested that royal orders had been obtained by 'slyly instilling' something into the king's ear; see the expression in T. Hearne, *Adami de Domerham Historia de Rebus Gestis Glastoniensibus*, I (Oxford, 1727), 306, A.D. 1126-35: 'precepto regis cujus auribus predictus Odo aliqua callide instillaverat'.

28 Van Caenegem, *Writs*, nr 16, p. 420, A.D. 1100-30.

29 W. H. Hart, *Historia et Cartularium monasterii Si Petri Gloucestriae*, Rolls Series, II (London, 1865), nr DXCIX, p. 108 (*Regesta Regum Anglo-Normannorum*, II, nr 1305, p. 167, A.D. 1120-1).

30 Barnes, 'The Anstey Case', p. 18 (A.D. 1159).

31 J. G. Jenkins, *The Cartulary of Missenden Abbey*, Historical Mss. Comm. J.P. 1, III (London, 1962), nr 818, pp. 188-9 (A.D. 1179-85) and G. H. Fowler, *Records of Harrold Priory*, Beds. Rec. Soc. (1935), nr 69*, pp. 55-6; cf. L. Milis, *L'Ordre des chanoines réguliers d'Arrouaise. Son histoire et son organisation, de la fondation de l'abbaye-mère (vers 1090) à la fin des chapitres annuels (1471)*, Rijksuniversiteit Gent. Werken Fac. Letteren, 147, I (Bruges, 1969), 290-2. Dr Milis is preparing an article on Harrold Priory in the period 1136-88.

32 L. Voss, *Heinrich von Blois, Bischof von Winchester (1129-71)*, Historische Studien, 210 (Berlin, 1932), IV d, 162-3 (A.D. 1169-71).

33 See an example of a purely executive papal order of restitution for an English beneficiary in Holtzmann, *Papsturkunden*, III, nr 39, pp. 162-163, A.D. 1142: 'Significatum nobis est quod Guilelmus filius Guarini ... ecclesiam...violenter detineat. Quocirca mandamus quatinus eundem Guillelmum ecclesiam...dimittere commoneas, quod si facere contempserit...coherceas' (Innocent II to Bishop Robert of Bath for Cirencester Abbey). Thus *c.* 1156-7 Archbishop Theobald wrote to Pope Adrian IV that on the basis of a papal mandate he had ordered Hugh of Dover to restore the church of Chilham to the monks of St Bertin. According to the monks they had been robbed *violenter et absque judicio*, and although Hugh promised to obey the order, he nevertheless argued his good right, stating – as Theobald reports, quoting his arguments at length – that 'the petitions addressed to the pope by the

monks were in many respects false' (W. J. Millor, H. E. Butler and C. N. L. Brooke, *The Letters of John of Salisbury* (London, 1955), I, nr 23, pp. 37–8).

34 C. R. Cheney, 'England and the Roman Curia under Innocent III', *Journal of Ecclesiastical History*, 18 (1967), 184. Professor Cheney points out (*ibid.*, p. 181) that in several bulls Innocent III admitted that he had been misled by deceitful suitors, see the Decretals of Gregory IX (I, III, 16, 17, 20, 22, 24, 37, 43); title III of Book I devoted to papal rescripts.

35 Holtzmann, *Papsturkunden*, I, nr 242, p. 531, A.D. 1186–7 ('a sede apostolica veritate tacita impetratas').

36 *Ibid.*, II, nr 445, pp. 538–9, A.D. 1193 ('per litteras apostolicas fraudulenter tacita veritate obtentas'); see a similar case in a letter of the same pope of 1197, *ibid.*, II, nr 283, p. 477.

37 *Ibid.*, II, nr. 214, pp. 407–8. The letter is concerned with the demand of Thomas Becket's creditors that his debts should be paid out of the revenues from his tomb.

38 *Ibid.*, nr 233, p. 363. Another striking case from *c.* 1175–85 concerns the nominee of Reiner the Fleming to the church of Wodeham, who being refused admission to the living by Archbishop Roger of York, went to Rome and returned with a mandate that he be admitted; if necessary, Bishop Hugh du Puiset of Durham was to eject the intruder and admit the plaintiff, after ascertaining the latter's fitness and the fact that the initial presentation had been to a vacant church (G. V. Scammell, *Hugh du Puiset, bishop of Durham* (Cambridge, 1956), p. 83). In one letter Alexander has to admit he has no recollection of taking a certain measure and he adds 'if we did, it arose from our being overworked' and Clement III admitted that 'because we cannot keep everything in mind, cases formerly committed to certain judges are committed straightway on the petition of other persons to other judges and so commission is frustrated by commission and the Roman Curia incurs the charge of levity', see Cheney, *From Becket to Langton*, p. 65. In the case between the archbishop and the monks of Canterbury Innocent III took firm action, and issued a mandate, that was found to contain five false statements and two suppressions of fact, because it was based on an ex parte statement from the monks (*op. cit.*, pp. 73–4).

39 The phrase occurs in a rescript of the Emperor Zeno of A.D. 477 (C. I, 23, 7).

40 A. van Hove, *De Rescriptis*, Commentarium Lovaniense in Codicem Iuris Canonici, I, IV (Malines, 1936), 132: 'In omnibus rescriptis subintelligenda est, etsi non expressa, conditio "si preces veritate nitantur"?' Already Gratian had said 'mendax enim precator debet carere impetratis' (dictum Gratiani post c. 16, C. XXV, q. ii). See on the clause 'si preces ...' and on the Roman process on rescripts M. Kaser, *Das römische Zivilprozessrecht* (Munich, 1966), pp. 520–4. This late Roman procedure was bedevilled by much the same pitfalls as appeared in the period under review, and caused by similar conditions (there was a special *praescriptio mendaciorum* for the losers under it).

41 Van Caenegem, *Writs*, nr 86, pp. 456–7; *Regesta Regum Anglo-Normannorum*, III, nr 545, p. 201, with the date 1143–7.

42 *Regesta Regum Anglo-Normannorum*, III, nr 546, p. 202, A.D. 1147–52. Professor Cronne rightly stresses the importance of Stephen's reign for legal developments (*Stephen*, pp. 219–20).

43 See Van Caenegem, *Writs*, nr 18 (*anno* 1155), 152 (*anno* 1155?), 91 (*anno* 1156 or 1158), 92 (*anno* 1158), 96 (*anno* 1155–66), 98 (*anno* 1166) and 94 (early Henry II).

44 A. Harding, *A Social History of English Law*, Penguin (Harmondsworth, 1966), p. 41.

45 Cam, *Law-Finders*, p. 213: 'By making himself the protector of the lawful possessor, great or small, the king had bound together the rights of ruler and subject.' The pipe rolls contain names of people punished for trying to bring the action who were not entitled to it (15 Henry II, 149: quia petierunt assisam sicut liberi et fuerunt rustici).

46 The indictment of criminals under the Assize of Clarendon was a public duty, through juries of presentment. So was the presentment of unlawful disseisins: we find hundreds and vills being amerced for concealing disseisins (Pipe Roll 14 Henry II, 133, 164ff). See similar fines for failure to present murderers under the Assize of Clarendon in 12 Henry II, 65, 76. The criminal beginnings of novel disseisin are a disputed question. However, the amercement of people for not accusing someone of unlawful disseisin in their district points in the direction of criminal repression rather than a purely civil action concerning private parties. Further arguments for the origin of novel disseisin as a criminal action are given in Milsom, *Historical Foundations*, pp. 117–18.

47 Doubt has recently been cast on the text of the Assize of Clarendon, but it has been vindicated with solid arguments by Holt, 'The Assizes of Henry II: the Texts', pp. 85–100.

48 They are described in Pipe Roll 12 Henry II as *dissaisina injusta* (p. 4), *d. super breve Regis* (7, 10), *d. super Assisam Regis* (65), *quia dissaisivit … injuste* (98) or just *dissaisina* (14). They come from Lincolnshire, Buckinghamshire, Rutland, Dorset and Somerset. It is true, as G. D. G. Hall remarks (*Eng. Hist. Rev.*, 76 (1961), 318) that the entry *pro dissaisina super assisam* appears in the early part of the account and not under *Nova Placita et Nove Conventiones*. However, Lady Stenton, *Pleas before the King*, III, p. cix, points out that in Pipe Roll 13 Henry II (1167) we find (belated) returns of the work done in 1166 in Northamptonshire by earl Geoffrey de Mandeville and Richard de Lucy, that are *not* put under the New Pleas heading; and she draws attention to other anomalies of that sort, in *English Justice*, p. 62: 'Walter of Gloucester appears as a forest judge only in Warwickshire with one debt recorded above and others below the "new pleas" heading,' and p. 64: 'Some of the debts imposed by Geoffrey in Essex and in Nottinghamshire and Derbyshire appear under the "new pleas" heading, but in all other shires they are entered above that heading and by later rules should represent debts incurred in previous years.' A comparable anomaly concerning the *placita curie per Rogerum Reinfridi et socios suos* in the Pipe Roll of 25 Henry II is pointed out in her *Pleas before the King*, III, p. lxi. In any case, the other entries in 12 Henry II of amercements for (unjust) disseisin (against the king's writ), which we have just seen, occur under the pleas of Geoffrey de Mandeville and Richard de Lucy, who were on eyre in 1166. A fundamental discussion of the eyre of 1166 can be found in Holt, 'The Assizes of Henry II: the Texts', pp. 101–6.

49 See the statistic of payments for unjust disseisins A.D. 1166–70 (with two late payments in the roll of 1171) in Van Caenegem, *Writs*, p. 285 (and graph, p. 296) and compare them with the chronology of the

general eyres as given in the previous chapter, pp. 20–2; see also the remarks of G. D. G. Hall in *Eng. Hist. Rev.* 76 (1961), 318

50 The general eyres were resumed in 1175 (on a reissue of the Assize of Clarendon?); in 1176 the justices were given a new set of instructions, the Assize of Northampton, which continued the work of that of Clarendon of 1166, but on an enlarged and more severe scale.

51 Payments *pro habenda assissa de terra* (of 1168), *pro recognitione de terra* (1170), *ut habeat recognitionem et saisinam* (1175) occur in the pipe rolls, see Van Caenegem, *Writs*, p. 294, cf. the statistic of payments for recognitions, p. 100: a considerable number first occurs in 1176 and 1177, in connection with the second wave of general eyres and fines for unlawful disseisin.

52 See references to lost enactments (*statutum, edictum, assisa, constitutio, stabilimentum*) of the early years of Henry II in England in Van Caenegem, *Writs*, pp. 217, 284, 331 and 338 and in Glanvill (XIII, 11, ed. Hall, p. 155, n. 3) (cf. Richardson and Sayles, *Law and Legislation*, p. 102), and in Normandy in J. Yver, 'Le "Très Ancien Coutumier" de Normandie, miroir de la législation ducale? Contribution à l'étude de l'ordre public normand à la fin du XIIe siècle', *Tijdschrift voor Rechtsgeschiedenis. Revue d'Histoire du Droit*, 39 (1971), 372–4. A good deal of research remains to be done on the technique and form of legislation. One way of introducing new rules, in England as elsewhere, was oral promulgation by the king (see p. 27, n. 69). Another was sending a writ to royal justices (see, for example, J. C. Robertson and J. B. Sheppard, *Materials for the history of Thomas Becket*, Rolls Series, VII (London, 1885), 147) or sheriffs (see, for example, J. C. Robertson, *op. cit.*, V (1881), 152); cf. Richardson and Sayles, *Governance*, pp. 307–8. For some of Henry's most important measures no official written enactment has survived and they are only reported in chronicles.

53 Stenton, *English Justice*, pp. 39–42.

54 Stubbs, *Select Charters*, p. 180, c. 5: Item Justitiae domini regis faciant fieri recognitionem de dissaisinis factis super Assisam, a tempore quo dominus rex venit in Angliam proximo post pacem factam inter ipsum et regem filium suum.

55 Recovery of *catalla et fructus* already in Glanvill, XIII, 38, 39, real damages from 1198 onwards, the amount being assessed together with the amercement (G. E. Woodbine, *Glanvill, De Legibus et consuetudinibus regni Angliae*, Yale Histor. Publ., Mss. and Texts, 13 (New Haven, 1932), 293).

56 There is the analogy with the prosecution under the Assize of Clarendon of serious crime committed after Henry II became king and the fact that we find the (first) coronation of Henry II in several actions in Glanvill (II, 3; IV, 6; XII, 11; XIII, 3–6), see Richardson and Sayles, *Law and Legislation*, p. 95, n. 2.

57 27 Henry II, pp. 26, 44.

58 Some such expressions were widely used in legal documents of the period, notably in papal letters for English beneficiaries. See 'injuste et per violentiam detinent' (Holtzmann, *Papsturkunden*, II, nr 22, pp. 165–7, A.D. 1139), 'sine ratione et judicio ablate' (*ibid.*, II, nr 33, p. 177, A.D. 1143), 'per violentiam et contra iustitiam' (II, nr 98, p. 283, A.D. 1158), 'sine iudicio et iustitia spoliati' (II, nr 146, p. 337, A.D. 1175), 'iniuste et absque ordine iudiciario spoliantur (I, nr 106, p. 370, A.D. 1167–9), 'absque ordine iudiciario spoliavit' (I, nr 169, p. 440, A.D. 1179).

59 We find the distinction between *possessio* and *proprietas* and the principle that after restoration of possession a plea on property can follow, in papal letters for England in the twelfth century, see Holtzmann, *Papsturkunden*, I, nr 23 p. 248 (*anno* 1141); II, nr 173, pp. 365–6 (*anno* 1178); III, nr 47, pp. 171–2 (*anno* 1145); III, nr 213, pp. 346–8 (*anno* 1174); III, nr 332, p. 445 (*anno* 1171–81); III, nr 380, pp. 482–7 (*anno* 1186). The rule *nemo placitet dissaisiatus* (*ante legitimam restitutionem*) is given repeatedly and with emphasis in the *Leges Henrici I*, well before Vacarius arrived in England with the *Corpus Juris* in his baggage (53, 3, 5, 6; 61, 21, ed. Liebermann, *Gesetze*, I, 574, 582).
60 See the numerous royal writs on seisin in Van Caenegem, *Writs*, nrs 52ff., from A.D. 1077 onwards, and the commentary, *ibid.*, pp. 267–83, also the remarks in Cronne, *Stephen*, p. 219, on the growing emphasis on seisin under Stephen and the rôle of the royal scribes in developing standard formulas for the writs. For an interesting case in the county of Flanders, long before any Bolognese influence, see F. L. Ganshof, 'Un cas précoce de distinction entre l'action possessoire et l'action pétitoire en Flandre', *Le Moyen Age* (1963), pp. 259–70 (A.D. 1116–32). In the thirteenth and following centuries several works on customary law have compared seisin–right and *possessio–proprietas* and applied Roman notions and terms to customary institutions.
61 The preoccupation with seisin as distinct from right was much older than the revival of Roman Law and its impact on England. Nothing in the action and writ of novel disseisin is Romano-canonical – neither its terminology, its procedure (least of all the essential rôle of the jury), the justices in eyre, nor the notion of seisin is typical for the procedure of the *ordines judiciarii*. See, however, a restatement of the old opinion that novel disseisin was the result of Roman Law influence in (F.) Joüon des Longrais, *Henry II and his justiciars had they a political plan in their reforms about seisin?* Lecture delivered at Gonville and Caius College, Cambridge 1961 (Paris, 1962), pp. 10–13.
62 F. Ruffini, *L'Actio spolii. Studio giuridico* (Turin, 1889), p. 303; Van Caenegem, *Writs*, pp. 386–90.
63 Glanvill says so repeatedly: 'After seisin has been fully recovered, the tenant who has lost seisin may contest the question of right by means of a writ of right' (XIII, 9, cf. also XIII, 20 and I, 16), although there are restrictions, for example in favour of a minor (in the writ of XIII, 14), where Glanvill states that 'in such a case, if seisin remains with the minor as the result of the assize, he shall not answer as to the question of right until he is of full age' (XIII, 15). This is rather different from considering the petty assizes as a preliminary to an action on right. Glanvill treats the two aspects as existing separately, different procedures about different things, see XIII, 1: 'So far the questions which most often arise in pleas about right (*de recto*) have been dealt with; there remain for discussion those which are concerned with seisin (*super saisinis*) only' – elsewhere he uses the terminology *possessio–proprietas* for seisin and right, e.g. in I, 3.
64 N. D. Hurnard, 'Did Edward I reverse Henry II's Policy upon Seisin?', *Eng. Hist. Rev.*, 69 (1954), 536, n. 3. Seisin and the Roman *possessio* were comparable but not similar, in spite of occasional attempts to use the Roman terminology to fit medieval feudal institutions; see F. Joüon des Longrais, *La conception anglaise de la saisine du XIIe au XIVe siècle*. Etudes de droit anglais, vol. 1 (Paris, 1924), p. 45 and

NOTES TO PAGES 45-6

T. F. T. Plucknett, *Legislation of Edward I*, Ford Lectures (Oxford, 1949), p. 53. Seisin was not necessarily connected with land, one could, for example, be in seisin of criminal jurisdiction. See the case of the abbot of St Edmund's Bury who, foreseeing a conflict with the archbishop of Canterbury, put himself in seisin by getting hold *manu militari* of certain criminals, saying: 'volo me ponere in saisinam hujus libertatis et post me defendam cum auxilio sancti Ædmundi cujus jus hoc est' (H. E. Butler, *The Chronicle of Jocelin of Brakelond* (London, 1949), pp. 50–3).

65 See the case of a certain Peter in the court of Archbishop Theobald in 1154–61, quoted by Lady Stenton (*English Justice*, p. 34) as showing that 'the King's mind was moving towards preliminary action concerning merely the seisin and not the right' and providing 'sufficient proof that at least six years before the critical date 1166 the King has commanded that a preliminary action which shall not bar a subsequent plea of right shall be heard in a lord's court'. Two remarks are called for. The judgment on seisin was given against Peter and for the canons of St Paul's because Peter had 'always failed in proof' and the canons 'are absolved from the petition of seisin which he – Peter – would have had if he had abounded in proof'; in other words Peter failed to prove his case and therefore lost his plea on seisin 'reserving nevertheless the question of right if Peter should think fit to plead it'. But his chances in a plea on right would be very slim, as he lacked proof. Can one imagine that he withheld some piece of evidence, thus losing a legal battle that lasted three years, in order to produce it in a second lawsuit? If he was really desperate, he could put his hopes on judicial combat in a plea on right, but who could afford the better champion, Peter or the canons of St Paul's? The latter, no doubt. The text does not speak of a 'preliminary' action, it just mentions the established notion that, theoretically at least, the loss of a plea on seisin did not preclude pleading on right. As the king merely issued a writ ordering Theobald to do right to the plaintiff on the question of seisin which he wanted to raise in the archbishop's court, there is nothing here to tell us in what way the king's mind was moving, since in those years it was becoming customary for plaintiffs to support their claim in lords' courts by bringing a royal writ.

66 Stenton, *English Justice*, p. 33.

67 Glanvill, XIII, 33: 'The king to sheriff, greeting. N. has complained to me that R. unjustly and without judgment has disseised him of his free tenement in such-and-such a vill since my last voyage to Normandy . . . And meanwhile you are to see that the tenement is viewed by twelve free and lawful men of the neighbourhood and their names endorsed on this writ and summon them . . . ready to make the recognition. And summon R. . . . to be there then to hear the recognition . . . and have there the summoners and this writ and the names of the sureties.'

68 See some possible reasons for this unfortunate gap in our source material in M. M. Bigelow, *History of Procedure in England from the Norman Conquest. The Norman Period (1066–1204)* (Boston, 1880), p. 170 and Stenton, *English Justice*, pp. 32–3: writs of right were in the hands of those who obtained them unless they gave them to their opponents as a sign of quitclaim. They therefore found their way into monastic collections of charters and cartularies and so were conserved. Returnable writs, although addressed to sheriffs, were returned to the

central courts and therefore not conserved locally; the earliest we have are naturally the oldest conserved in the central archives and they unfortunately do not take us beyond the very last years of the twelfth century, hence a fatal gap for the study of the wording of the Common Law writs between the early years of Henry II and Glanvill.

69 J. Yver, 'Le Bref Anglo-Normand', *Tijdschr. v. Rechtsgeschiedenis. Rev. d'Hist. du Droit*, 29 (1961), 324. The text of the Norman writ is (*Très Ancien Coutumier*, LXXIII, 2): Rex vel senescallus baillivo de tali loco, salutem. Precipe H. quod sine dilatione resaisiat R. de tenemento suo apud talem locum, unde saisitus fuit ultimo augusto (vel pre-ultimo), et unde postea eum dissaisivit injuste et sine judicio. Quod nisi fecerit ... tunc submone XII legales milites et homines de visineto quod sint ... parati juramento inde facere recognitionem et interim terram illam videri facias ... et submone predictum H. quod sit ad visionem et ad assisiam ...

70 Papal letters for England beginning with 'conquestus est' in Holtzmann, *Papsturkunden*, I, nr 169, p. 440 (A.D. 1179: 'conquestus est nobis O. clericus quod cum ... idem S. ... predictum O. predicta ecclesia absque ordine iudiciario spoliavit ... mandamus quatinus ...); I, nr 204, p. 475 (A.D. 1181); II, nr 36, p. 185 (A.D. 1144); III, nr 47, pp. 171–2 (A.D. 1145). The formula does exceptionally occur in early writs of Henry II, see 'Conquesti sunt mihi monachi de Rading ...' in Van Caenegem, *Writs*, nr 93, p. 460 (*anno* 1154–61).

71 I have in my *Royal Writs* collected numerous documents to illustrate the distant origin and gradual development of notions and practices that led to the Common Law actions, grouped under such titles as 'writ of right' or 'writ of novel disseisin' and with the warning that I was only 'assembling for each of the main writs of the early common law, a set of eleventh- and twelfth-century "precursors", in order to illustrate its origins and first developments'. However certain historians, who have not noticed this explanation on p. 405 and have read 'writs of novel disseisin' where the heading is in fact 'writ of novel disseisin', were shocked to find that 'writs of Novel Disseisin and of Mort d'Ancestor, were classified as such, since the Conquest of England by William the Conqueror' (Joüon des Longrais, *Henry II and his justiciars*, p. 7; cf. a similar misapprehension in Cronne, *Stephen*, p. 259); had I said this, they would have been justified. Professor Cronne (*Stephen*, pp. 258–9, 262), is, however, hesitant: he admits that 'it is not at all difficult to find in Stephen's reign and in those of his three Norman predecessors royal writs which seem to adumbrate some of the famous writs of Henry II's time' and that the writs of Henry I and Stephen 'helped enormously by their practical effects to establish the foundations and create the assumptions upon which later evocatory procedure could be firmly based'. But he thinks nevertheless that 'to read our history backward by taking the stereotyped writs we find in Glanvill and seeking their earlier prototypes among the writs of Henry II's predecessors is a dangerous historical method' since 'an attempt to judge the intention of the earlier by the later writs may lead to false conclusions'. It is clear that the Norman kings did not order right to be done or seisin to be restored with the intention that this would eventually lead to the rise of the Common Law, but history is full of initiatives that eventually led to unforeseen results.

72 I am referring to chapter IV: 'The Writ Process', of his *History of Pro-*

cedure, pp. 147–200. It is true that the chapter is more interesting for the material it contains than for the systematic treatment of the subject, but it contains important ideas on the gradual development of the writs, 'not created by a stroke of the pen' (p. 147), 'out of rough and even shapeless material' (*ibid.*), on the rôle of the earlier 'writs of execution' (pp. 153, 155), on 'Glanvill's writ of novel disseisin as a development in regular course from older material' (p. 170) and as 'no essential innovation upon the ancient procedure' (p. 175, cf. pp. 182 and 192 in the same sense).

73 Van Caenegem, *Writs*, pp. 168–72; Stenton, *English Justice*, p. 28.

74 Glanvill carefully points out that whoever lost a tenement in mort d'ancestor could always try to win it back by a plea on right. The numerous actions of mort d'ancestor resulting in final concords show however, how definite this 'possessory assize' tended in fact to be.

75 The initial time limit which was the first coronation of Henry II (1154), was pushed forward from time to time, for example, to the first coronation of Richard I (1189) and so on.

76 Stubbs, *Select Charters*, pp. 179–80.

77 'The king to the sheriff, greeting. If G., son of O. gives you security for prosecuting his claim, then summon by good summoners twelve free and lawful men of the vicinity of such a vill to be before me or my justices on such a day, ready to recognize under oath whether O., the father of the aforesaid G., was seized in his demesne as of his fee of one virgate of land in that vill on the day he died, whether he died after my first coronation, and whether the said G. is his next heir.' The sheriff is also told to let the jurors view the land, to endorse their names on the writ, to summon R., who holds the land, to appear at the recognition and to be there with the summoners and the writ (XIII, 3). Glanvill also gives variations in case the father's going on a pilgrimage or a crusade or putting on the habit of religion is claimed by the heir, or in case the heir is under age; for novel disseisin too variants according to different circumstances and specific forms of nuisance were devised and given in Glanvill (XIII, 33ff.).

78 Earliest payments *pro recognitione de laico feodo* and the like in Pipe Roll 27 Henry II, p. 57 (*anno* 1181), 30 Henry II, p. 8 (*anno* 1184).

79 See a case in Luton in 1138 in T. Walsingham, *Gesta Abbatum monasterii Sancti Albani*, ed. H. T. Riley, Rolls Series, I (London, 1867), 113–115; cf. L. F. R. Williams, 'William the Chamberlain and Luton Church', *Engl. Hist. Rev.* 28 (1913), 719–30. The jury found that the land in dispute had always been *libera elemosina* until William the Chamberlain turned the *ecclesiastica libertas* into a *servicium militare* and judgment was given against him.

80 Except if it was lay fee and both parties claimed to hold of the same bishop or baron, in which case the plea belonged to his court. No change in seisin was allowed at this preliminary stage (Stubbs, *Select Charters*, pp. 165–6). The assumption that cl. 9 of the Constitutions of Clarendon reveals the existence of the writ *utrum* is rightly criticized by W. L. Warren in a review in *History*, 52 (1967), 172–3; Lady Stenton's tendency to place the creation of various Common Law writs early in Henry II's reign is also criticized. Cl. 9 deals with the problem of competence and with the mode of proof (a jury before the chief justiciar), not with the way procedure was initiated and it is likely, as W. L.

Warren suggests, that *utrum* became a writ-process afterwards, like the other petty assizes.

81 Glanvill, XIII, 24: 'The king to the sheriff, greeting. Summon by good summoners twelve free and lawful men from the neighbourhood of such a vill to be before me or my justices on a certain day, ready to declare on oath whether one hide of land, which N. parson of the church in that vill claims as free alms of his church against R. in that vill, is the lay fee of R. or ecclesiastical fee. And meanwhile let them view the land . . .'; if it was judged to be ecclesiastical land, it owed no payment or service (other than religious) and the full income was for the church and parson.

82 J. Yver, 'Autour de l'absence d'avouerie en Normandie', *Bull. Soc. Antiquaires Normandie*, 57 (1965), 257.

83 Mansi, *Amplissima Collectio*, XXII, col. 227, c. 17. For interesting examples of pensions paid by rectors of churches to the patrons who presented them, see H. Mayr-Harting, *The Acta of the Bishops of Chichester 1075–1207* (Torquay, 1964), nr 117, p. 1070, A.D. 1180–6 and nr 134, p. 185, A.D. 1187–97.

84 This clause was intended to exclude the 'Anarchy' under Stephen, see Painter, *English feudal barony*, p. 35. It is absent from the writ in Glanvill (XIII, 19), although he mentions it in IV, 1, but occurs in the oldest surviving writs of 1199 and in the cases on the early plea rolls (Stenton, *Pleas before the King*, I, Selden Soc. vol. 67 (London, 1952), nr 3497, p. 373, nr 3533, p. 402, nr 3534, p. 403; C. T. Flower, *Introduction to the Curia Regis Rolls, A.D. 1199–1230*, Selden Soc. vol. 62 (London, 1944), pp. 168ff.

85 Juries had already decided on advowson by royal command, see a case in Derby in 1156–7 (R. R. Darlington, *The cartulary of Darley abbey*, Derb. Arch. Soc. (Kendal, 1945), nr A 12, p. 71). In the Constitutions of Clarendon, c. 1 Henry II claimed litigation on advowson for his court.

86 It should not be forgotten that exceptions could be pleaded on points of law or fact, avoiding the injustice caused by too formal and mechanistic an application of the terms of the assizes.

87 See on the significance of cl. 34: N. D. Hurnard, 'Magna Carta, clause 34', *Studies M. Powicke* (Oxford, 1948), pp. 157–79; M. T. Clanchy, 'Magna Carta, Clause Thirty-Four', *Eng. Hist. Rev.* 79 (1964), 542–8; Glanvill, ed. Hall, pp. 179–80; Stenton, *English Justice*, pp. 78–9.

88 'The king to the sheriff, greeting. Command N. to render R. justly and without delay one hide of land in such a vill, which the said R. complains that the aforesaid N. is withholding from him. If he does not do so, summon him by good summoners to be before me or my justices on the day after the octave of Easter, to show why he has not done so. And have there the summoners and this writ' (I, 6).

89 *Regesta Regum Anglo-Normannorum*, I, nr 368a, *anno* 1094–5 : Hugh the larderer is to restore a portion of fish to the abbey of Battle.

90 *Regesta Regum Anglo-Normannorum*, I, nr 459, *anno* 1089–1100; see more examples in Van Caenegem, *Writs*, p. 240.

91 Van Caenegem, *Writs*, nr 37, p. 430, see also p. 239, n. 1 (A.D. 1112 or 1113).

92 Stevenson, *Abingdon*, II, 123.

93 *Regesta Regum Anglo-Normannorum*, III, nr 257, p. 92, cf. Cronne, *Stephen*, pp. 259–60. The trouble with Heatherslaw was not over yet under Henry II, who sent some stern writs to Cecily de Muschamp and

her son Thomas, expressing 'astonishment and great displeasure that they had not yet done what he told them in his other writs concerning the manor of Heatherslaw', Van Caenegem, *Writs*, nrs 47, 47*a*, p. 435.

94 H. E. Salter, *The Thame Cartulary*, Oxon. Rec. Soc. 25 (Oxford, 1947), nr 49, p. 45, *c*. A.D. 1180 : William son of Geoffrey restores land to Thame abbey 'ad mandatum domini regis'. The mere fact of not doing what a royal writ ordered was promptly punished, thus 'Petrus de Gollinton debet 40s. quia non fecit preceptum Regis per breve ipsius' (Pipe Roll 12 Henry II, 57).

95 Stevenson, *Abingdon*, II, 123.

96 See a writ of Stephen to Roger Little in favour of the abbey of Gloucester, ordering him to leave land in Quedgeley in peace 'desicut abbas dicit quod rectum in ea non habes', or else to go to court, *Regesta Regum Anglo-Normannorum*, III, nr 355, p. 135, *anno* 1135–9.

97 Henry I orders the barons of Bury St Edmunds to come to the abbot's pleas 'et non remaneant pro ullo breve quod habent ut non veniant, *Regesta Regum Anglo-Normannorum*, II, nr 181, *anno* 1100–33.

98 *Regesta Regum Anglo-Normannorum*, III, nr 355, p. 135, 1135–9: the addressee is either to give up the land in Quedgeley altogether or to go to the court of the abbot of Gloucester and try and deraign it there. Something vaguely resembling this can be found in a writ of William the Conqueror for Ramsey in which he ordered generally that whatever land (in the time of troubles after 1066) had been taken from the abbey was to be restored unless it could be deraigned in the chapter court, Macray, *Chronicon abbatiae Rameseiensis* (London, 1886), pp. 205–6; *Regesta Regum Anglo-Normannorum*, I, nr 177, 1070–82.

99 Farrer, *Early Yorkshire Charters*, III (Edinburgh, 1916), nr 1301, p. 28, with the date 1112–22: *Regesta Regum Anglo-Normannorum*, II, nr 1311, p. 169, with the date 1112–21.

100 Van Caenegem, *Writs*, nr 180, p. 507.

101 *Regesta Regum Anglo-Normannorum*, III, nr 692, p. 255. To the judicialization of the writs one might apply the words of Lord Devlin about certain institutions of criminal procedure, which 'were all born from the womb of the executive'; of the writs, as of criminal procedure, one might say that 'there is a constant drift, always in the same direction, from unfettered administrative action to regulated judicial proceeding' and 'change from the administrative to the judicial and from what is discretionary to what is obligatory' (P. Devlin, *The criminal prosecution in England* (London, 1960), pp. 2 and 10).

102 *Praecipe quod reddat* for land (I, 6) and for advowson (IV, 2), *praecipe* for dower *unde nihil habet* (VI, 15), for fine not observed (VIII, 4), for receiving homage and relief (IX, 5), *praecipe quod reddat* for debt (X, 2), *praecipe* against debtor's surety for debt (X, 4), for debt secured by gage (X, 7) and *praecipe quod reddat* for land gaged, or writ of gage (X, 9).

103 See, for example, nr 197 in The Luffield Register, De Haas and Hall, *Early Registers of Writs*, p. 95.

104 In *sur disseisin* there was a flaw from the start; here the situation started regularly enough, but went wrong in course of time : 'The king to the sheriff, greeting. Command N. to restore justly and without delay so much land [or, certain specified land] in such a vill to R., who gaged it to him for 100 marks until the end of a term which is now past, as R. alleges; and to accept payment from him (or, which he alleges he

128

has redeemed by payment). If he does not do so, summon him by good summoners to be before me or my justices at a certain place on a certain day to show why he has not done so. And have there the summoners and this writ.'

105 Bracton, fol. 413b.

106 This is a writ *praecipe* for land including the words 'et tenere de nobis in capite' or 'tenere de domino rege'. We find it in the earliest registers of writs, for example in the Irish Register of 1227, c. 4 (De Haas and Hall, *Early Registers*, p. 2), the Pre-Mertonian Register, of the 1220s, c. 3 (*ibid.*, p. 18) and the Luffield Register, of the 1260s, c. 90 (*ibid.*, p. 37).

107 See the writ in the Luffield Register, c. 8 (*ibid.*, p. 36); the full clause reads 'quia talis capitalis dominus feodi illius remisit nobis inde curiam suam'.

108 Already in the thirteenth century cl. 34 was understood as having this limited application. For M. T. Clanchy's article, see p. 50, n. 87.

109 Van Caenegem, *Writs*, nr 66, pp. 445-6, writ of William Rufus, of A.D. 1093-7.

110 See, for example, such a writ of Henry I for Abingdon of A.D. 1105 (?) in Van Caenegem, *Writs*, nr 108, p. 469.

111 See Stephen's writ of 1143-54 in *Regesta Regum Anglo-Normannorum*, III, nr 552, p. 204.

112 Van Caenegem, *Writs*, nrs 114-20, 122-4, pp. 472-7; writ nr 121, p. 476 is an order to a landowner to send back the fugitive serfs of the abbot of Holme, who had run away since Henry I's death; if necessary, the sheriff of Norfolk should see that the order is carried out.

113 Glanvill, XII, 11; the wording of the writ is conservative, using traditional phrases.

114 He might have fallen into the hands of another Osbert de Torp' who accounted for 15 marks (in Pipe Roll 21 Henry II, p. 178, *anno* 1175) 'because he incarcerated a man whom he wanted to prove was a villein and he could not'. The plea on status was difficult, see Poole, *Obligations of Society*, pp. 12-34 and Glanvill, V, 3, 4 : the verdict of the neighbourhood was resorted to and battle expressly excluded. See the remarks on villeinage in Richardson and Sayles, *Law and Legislation*, pp. 138-49.

115 Glanvill, V, 2: 'The king to the sheriff, greeting. R., who claims to be a free man has complained to me that N. seeks to reduce him to villein status. Therefore I command you, if the aforesaid R. gives you security for prosecuting his claim, to transfer that plea [at present in the hands of the sheriff on the basis of a writ of naifty] before me or my justices on such a day and to see that he goes in peace meanwhile; and summon the aforesaid N. by good summoners to be there then, to show why he unjustly seeks to reduce him to villein status, and have there the summoners and this writ.' The king suspends his own writ of naifty and offers the alleged villein a hearing in his court. The wording of this writ is quite recent. If there was no discussion about the unfree status of the fugitive, but two masters claimed him, the dispute was left for the sheriff to settle in the county court: the king's court was only concerned with people who were or claimed to be free.

116 See p. 52, n. j.

117 Pollock and Maitland, *History of English Law*, II, 512.

118 Magna Carta, c. 20. See the interesting chapter V, 'Amercements', in

Poole, *Obligations of Society*, pp. 77–91 and Pollock and Maitland, *op. cit.*, II, 513 : the lawful men of the neighbourhood by whose oath the amercements were 'affeered' clearly were an assessing jury.

119 See the discussion of certain early, but inconclusive texts in the following chapter, p. 83, nn. 58–60.

120 Its date is obscure; it appears in the Exchequer Roll of 1180, but it may be a good deal older because of the use of the archaic term *jurea* instead of *recognitio*.

121 In England pleading on advowson was also claimed for the king's court, see p. 16.

122 J. R. Strayer, 'The Writ of Novel Disseisin in Normandy at the End of the Thirteenth Century', *Medieval Statecraft and the Perspectives of History* (Princeton, 1971), pp. 3–12 (a slightly revised version of a paper published in 1937); R. Besnier, '"Inquisitiones" et "Recognitiones". Le nouveau système des preuves à l'époque des Coutumiers normands', *Rev. hist. droit français et étranger*, 4th ser., 28 (1950), 183–212; id., 'Le procès pétitoire dans le droit normand du XIIe et du XIIIIe siècle, *ibid.*, 30 (1952), 195–222; Id., 'Le procès possessoire dans le droit normand du XIIe et du XIIIe siècle', *ibid.*, 31 (1953), 378–408; id., La dégénérescence des caractères normands des preuves dans la procédure civile du duché après la rédaction du Grand Coutumier', *ibid.*, 37 (1959), 48–61; J. Yver, 'Le Bref anglo-normand', pp. 313–30; id., 'Le "Très Ancien Coutumier" de Normandie'. I am very grateful to Professor Yver, of Caen, who is preparing a study on the Norman writ system and most generously advised me for the paragraphs on Normandy.

123 Southern, *Western Society and the Church*, p. 111.

124 W. J. La Due, *Papal Rescripts of Justice and English Royal Procedural Writs, 1150–1250. A Comparative Study. An Excerpt*, Pontificia Universitas Lateranensis. Institutum Utriusque Juris. Theses, ad Lauream, 155 (Rome, 1960). The author deals essentially with rescripts for judges delegate.

125 See pp. 35–8.

126 G. Barraclough, 'Audientia Litterarum Contradictarum', Dictionnaire de Droit canonique, I (Paris, 1935), cols. 1387–99; Herde, *Beiträge zum päpstlichen Kanzlei- und Urkundenwesen im dreizehnten Jahrhundert*, Münchener Hist. Studien. Abt. Gesch. Hilfswiss., 1 (Kallmünz, 1961), pp. 164–73; id., 'Papal formularies for letters of justice (13th–16th centuries)', *Proc. Sec. Internat. Cong. Medieval Canon Law* (Vatican, 1965), pp. 321–45; id., 'Ein Formelbuch Gerhards von Parma mit Urkunden des Auditor litterarum contradictarum aus dem Jahre 1277', *Archiv für Diplomatik*, 13 (1967), 225–312; id., *Audientia Litterarum Contradictarum. Untersuchungen über die päpstlichen Justizbriefe und die päpstliche Delegationsgerichtsbarkeit vom 13. bis zum Beginn des 16. Jahrhunderts*, I, Bibliothek des Deutschen Historischen Instituts in Rom, 31 (Tübingen, 1970), 20–74, 181–232; J. E. Sayers, *Papal Judges delegate in the Province of Canterbury 1198–1254. A Study in Ecclesiastical Jurisdiction and Administration* (Oxford, 1971), pp. 9–24. The court of Auditors, later named Rota, is a distinct if comparable thirteenth-century development. Its origins are older, but obscure; it was a court for the hearing of important cases before the pope in Rome.

127 *English Justice*, p. 53.

CHAPTER 3   PAGES 62–84

1 W. Nelson, *The Law of Evidence* (1717); G. Gilbert, *The Law of Evidence* (Dublin, 1754); S. M. Phillips, *A Treatise on the Law of Evidence* (London, 1815); J. Stephen, *A Digest of the Law of Evidence* (London, 1876); J. Thayer, *A Preliminary Treatise on Evidence at the Common Law* (Cambridge, Mass., 1898).

2 See the vast collection of studies both historical and ethnological in the volumes on *La Preuve*, published in the *Recueils de la Société Jean Bodin*, vols. 16–19, Brussels, 1963–5, as follows: Première partie: Antiquité (16, 1964), Deuxième Partie: Moyen Age et Temps Modernes (17, 1965), Troisième Partie: Civilisations archaïques, asiatiques et islamiques (18, 1963), Quatrième partie: Période contemporaine (19, 1963).

3 See our general outline, 'La preuve dans le droit du moyen âge occidental', *Recueils de la Société Jean Bodin*, 17, *La Preuve*, II (Brussels, 1965), 691–753 (with maps between pp. 430 and 431).

4 Text in Stubbs, *Select Charters*, p. 98; see some remarks in Stenton, *English Justice*, p. 6; Richardson and Sayles, *Law and Legislation*, p. 30.

5 F. L. Ganshof, 'La preuve dans le droit franc', *Recueils de la Société Jean Bodin*, 17, *La Preuve*, II (Brussels, 1965), 80, n. 25.

6 See the suggestion of a possibility in this sense, based on passages from *Beowulf*, and the *Battle of Maldon*, in M. W. Bloomfield, 'Beowulf, Byrhtnoth, and the Judgment of God: Trial by Combat in Anglo-Saxon England', *Speculum*, 44 (1969), 545–59.

7 In Scandinavia the duel was popular until the tenth century. In Denmark it was replaced by the ordeal of hot iron, which a Christian missionary was said to have undergone successfully; in A.D. 1000 judicial combat was forbidden in Iceland and in 1014 in Norway, in the wake of Christianity. The other ordeals were known among the north Germanic peoples, but were not so widespread as elsewhere, see H. Nottarp, *Gottesurteilstudien*, Bamberger Abhandlungen und Forschungen, 2 (Munich, 1956), 69–73.

8 J. Stevenson, *Libellus de vita et miraculis sancti Godrici, auctore Reginaldo Dunelmensi*, Surtees Soc., 20 (London, 1847), cap. CXV, §221, pp. 235–6.

9 *The History of Reynard the Fox, translated and printed by William Caxton in 1481*, ed. by D. B. Sands (Cambridge, Mass., 1960), pp. 46–7: 'Whereupon was a day set and was judged that Reynard should come and have excused him hereof and sworn on the holy saints that he was not guilty thereof. And when the book with the saints was brought forth [the original verses 82–3 say 'as soon as the saints were brought'], tho had Reynard bethought him otherwise and went his way again into his hole as he had nought set thereby.' See F. R. Jacoby, *Van den Vos Reinaerde. Legal elements in a Netherlands epic of the thirteenth century* (Munich, 1970).

10 Ed. J. Karacsonyi and S. Borovszky, *Regestrum varadiense examinum ferri candentis* (Budapest, 1903), see I. Zajtay, 'Le Registre de Varad. Un monument judiciaire du début du XIIIe siècle', *Rev. hist. de droit français et étranger*, 4th ser., 32 (1954), 527–62.

11 Van Caenegem, 'La preuve au moyen âge occidental', 699–700.

12 See an Anglo-Norman *Benedictio scuti et baculi ad duellum faciendum* from A.D. 1067–1130 in Liebermann, *Gesetze*, I, 430–1.

13 *Ibid.*, pp. 401–30.
14 Ed. K. Zeumer, *Formulae Merovingici et Karolini Aevi*, M.G.H., LL. V (1886), 599–722; see C. von Schwerin, 'Rituale für Gottesurteile', *Sitzungsberichte der Heidelberger Akademie der Wissenschaften, Phil.-hist. Kl.* (1932–3), 3. Abh.
15 Deut. 6: 16 and Matt. 4: 7. See for all this Nottarp, *Gottesurteilstudien*, pp. 255–62. A collection of relevant texts will be found in P. Browe, *De ordaliis*, I: *Decreta pontificum Romanorum et synodorum;* II: *Ordo et rubricae. Acta et facta. Sententiae*, Textus et documenta. Series theol. IV, 11 (Rome, 1932–3). The idea of the 'tempting of God' was the official reason for the prohibition by the Fourth Lateran Council and is quoted by authors in later centuries.
16 J. W. Baldwin, 'The intellectual preparation for the canon of 1215 against ordeals', *Speculum*, 36 (1961), 628ff.; id., *Masters, Princes and Merchants: The Social Views of Peter the Chanter and his Circle*, I (Princeton, 1970), 323–32.
17 There were references among civilians to judicial combat, notably under the influence of Lombard Law and of the misunderstood *crimen perduellionis* in Inst. 3, 1, 5; see a recent note by G. D'Amelio, 'Notizie di letteratura longobardistica', *Università di Cagliari. Studi Economico-Giuridici*, 46 (1969–70), 108–16, concerning the anonymous treatise *de pugna*.
18 Galbert of Bruges, *De multro . . . Karoli Comitis*, ed. H. Pirenne (Paris, 1891), c. 87, 105, 108, pp. 132, 150, 154–5 (for 1128, concerning Lambert of Aardenburg, who had taken part in the conspiracy against count Charles the Good of Flanders); *Sigeberti Continuatio Aquicinctina*, ed. D. Bethmann, M.G.H., SS. VI, 421, *anno* 1183 (the case of heretics accused at Ypres and Arras in 1183, who had confessed their sin – to a priest? – and went to the ordeal of fire, according to the canons of the council of Rheims of 1157, and were all successful).
19 Eadmer, *Historia Novorum in Anglia*, ed. M. Rule, Rolls Series (London, 1884), p. 102. The king is reported to have exclaimed: 'Quid est hoc? Deus est justus judex? Pereat qui deinceps hoc crediderit.'
20 The Assize of Clarendon names thieves, robbers and murderers and those who shelter them, the Assize of Northampton adds falsification and arson; Stubbs, *Select Charters*, pp. 170, 179.
21 The Assize of Clarendon calls them 'illi qui facient legem suam et mundi erunt per legem', *lex* being a usual term for an ordeal, *loc. cit.*, p. 172, c. 14; the Assize of Northampton calls the successful man 'ad aquam mundus' (c. 1, *ibid.*, p. 179).
22 Clarendon speaks of 'publice et turpiter diffamati testimonio multorum et legalium hominum' (c. 14, *ibid.*, p. 172), Northampton of 'retatus de murdro vel alia turpi felonia per commune comitatus et legalium militum patriae' (c. 1, *ibid.*, p. 179).
23 H. Pirenne and G. Espinas, 'Les coutumes de la gilde marchande de Saint-Omer', *Le Moyen Age* (1901), p. 1.
24 Ed. F. Vercauteren, *Chartes des comtes de Flandre 1071–1128* (Brussels, 1938), nr 45, p. 12. See on Flemish borough charters before 1200: R. C. van Caenegem, 'Coutumes et législation en Flandre aux XIe et XIIe siècles, *Les Libertés urbaines et rurales du XIe et au XIVe siècle* (Brussels, 1968), pp. 245–79. In England too a number of towns obtained exemption from judicial combat, see Bigelow, *History of Procedure*, p. 296.

25 See the maps quoted above, p. 64, n. 3. For the history of ordeals in Europe one should always consult H. Nottarp's encyclopedic *Gottesurteilstudien*.

26 F. Joüon des Longrais, 'La preuve en Angleterre', *Recueils de la Société Jean Bodin*, 17, *La Preuve*, II (Brussels, 1965), 217–18. One is reminded of Innocent III condemning as unreasonable the custom prevalent in the diocese of Passau, whereby in ecclesiastical cases the decision of the whole assembly – both literate and illiterate – was treated as final, see Cheney, *From Becket to Langton*, p. 156.

27 Besnier, 'La dégénérescence', pp. 48–61; Strayer, 'The Writ of Novel Disseisin in Normandy', pp. 3–12.

28 See Van Caenegem, *Writs*, pp. 94–103.

29 See, for example, a writ by Henry II to the sheriff of Lincolnshire 'Precipio tibi quod sine dilatione facias recognosci per sacramentum legalium civium Linc ...' (Van Caenegem, *Writs*, p. 462, nr 96, A.D. 1155–66); see comparable writs there p. 485, nr 138, p. 489, nr 147, p. 490, nr 148 ('fac recognosci per homines hundredi'), p. 423, nr 23 ('praecipio quod sine dilatione facias recognosci per sacramentum legalium hominum hundredi'). We find more general authorizations to certain landowners to organize recognitions if they want to, see, for example, a writ for Christ Church Canterbury of A.D. 1173 (?) in Van Caenegem, *Writs*, p. 463, nr 99.

30 A jury can be defined as a body of sworn people who give a formal answer to a question submitted to them concerning a fact, a right or a person in their neighbourhood. In the period under review their task of finding and giving a verdict was known as *recognoscere* and *recognitio*. The panel itself was known as the *juratores* or even the *recognitio*: when the jury met in the scope of the grand or petty assizes it was called an assize, *assisa*; *jurata* was another sort of jury, dealing with incidental questions arising in the course of litigation and the term is much younger. When used in a technical sense, *inquisitio* was the name of the royal inquest which led to a recognition by a jury: impanelling and interrogation of the jury was the *inquisitio*, the ensuing verdict was the *recognitio*.

31 Richardson and Sayles, *Law and Legislation*, p. 117.

32 See H. Brunner, *Die Entstehung der Schwurgerichte* (Berlin, 1871), pp. 84–126; Besnier, ' "Inquisitiones" et "Recognitiones" ', pp. 185–90; Ganshof, 'La preuve dans le droit franc', pp. 92–8. For a recent reappraisal see J. P. Dawson, *A History of Lay Judges* (Cambridge, Mass., 1960), pp. 119–22.

33 C. H. Haskins, *Norman Institutions* (Cambridge, Mass., 1918). pp. 232–4; J. Yver, 'Le Bref Anglo-Normand', p. 314. The Normans also introduced their ordeals in Sicily, see Nottarp, *Gottesurteilstudien*, p. 73.

34 In the charter of William the Conqueror of 1070–9 for the abbey of Fontenay, founded c. 1047 by Raoul Taisson, we read, in a very clear reference to a sworn inquest at the duke's command, 'cumque coepissent aliqui ex baronibus honoris abbati praedicto injurias facere et ea quae iste Radulfus Taxo et pater ejus huic ecclesiae dederant velle retrahere et hoc ad notitiam Willelmi regis praedicti pervenisset, nolens imminui quae consilio ejus et nutu antea facta fuerant, praecepit Ricardo vicecomiti Abrincarum quatinus de parte ejusdem regis ante se et Willelmum abbatem Cadomensem praedictaque Mathilde jubente barones honoris in Cadomo convenire jussisset et omnia quae praedicti

duo Radulfi Taxones huic Fontanensi ecclesiae dederant, sacramento super sanctum Evangelium facto, veraciter recordari fecisset, quod et factum est. Itum fuit Cadomum juxta praeceptum regis et electi sunt quatuor legitimi viri communi assensu, qui omnia haec quae praedicta sunt recordati sunt et se illa verissime recordatos fuisse super sanctum Evangelium juraverunt' – then four names are given (ed. *Gallia Christiana*, XI (1759), *Instrumenta*, col. 65 and P. de Farcy, *Abbayes de l'évêché de Bayeux*, I, *Cerisy, Cordillon, Fontenay, Longues* (Laval, 1887), p. 33) – *Regesta Regum Anglo-Normannorum*, I, nr 117, pp. 30–1 [A.D. 1070–9]. See Haskins, *Norman Institutions*, pp. 222–3 and R. V. Turner, 'The origins of the medieval English Jury', *Journal of British Studies*, 7 (1968), 6, who also refers to a case in Léchaudé-d'Anisy, *Grands Rôles des Echiquiers de Normandie*, Soc. des Antiquaires de Normandie, Documents historiques, I (Paris, 1845), 196–7; however, the phrase 'affuerunt etiam antiquissimi homines qui hoc viderant et audierant, parati probare secundum judicium regis quod nos edisseramus' does not necessarily refer to a jury.

35 M. Fauroux, *Recueil des actes des ducs de Normandie de 911 à 1066*, Mémoires de la Société des Antiquaires de Normandie, tom. XXXVI (Caen, 1961).

36 Yver, *Bref Anglo-Normand*, p. 317.

37 As I had spent a considerable time checking Brunner's material and looking for more in libraries and archives in England and France, I was surprised to read (Stenton, *English Justice*, p. 15) that I appear to accept 'without question', like Haskins before me, 'the doctrine so successfully taught by Brunner in 1871'.

38 F. Liebermann, *Gesetze*, I, 228–33; D. Whitelock, *English Historical Documents*, English Historical Documents, ed. D. C. Douglas, I: c. 500–1042 (London, 1955), 402–5 (with the date 978–1008). This code, III Æthelred, is mainly concerned with an area of the Danelaw, the Five Boroughs; there was another code issued at Woodstock, probably about the same time, concerning 'the law of the English'. The purpose of the Wantage Code was to record the assent of the king and his council to a regional customary law, relating especially to the keeping of the peace; see F. M. Stenton, *Anglo-Saxon England*, The Oxford History of England, ed. G. N. Clark, 3rd ed (Oxford, 1971), pp. 510, 651, who accepts the Scandinavian nature of this institution and points out the absence of the jury in 'pure Old English law'. The traditional date of 997 for the Code of Wantage is that of an assembly held at Wantage in that year, but there may, of course, have been other meetings of the *witan* at Wantage.

39 *Law and Legislation*, p. 25.

40 J. Raine, *Historiae Dunelmensis scriptores tres*, Surtees Soc. (London, 1839), nr 23, p. xxxi: *Regesta Regum Anglo-Normannorum*, II, nr 660, p. 35.

41 Hereford Cartulary, Oxford, Bodleian Library, Ms. Rawlinson B 329, fol. 137*v*.

42 Reading Cartulary, London, British Museum, Ms. Egerton 3031, fols. 41*v*–42 and Reading Cart., *ibid.*, Vespasian E XXV, fols. 68–68*v*.

43 Godstow Cartulary, London, Public Record Office, E 164/20, fol. 142.

44 Southwick Cartulary, Ms. Winchester, Hampshire Record Office, fols. 23*v*–24. On this and the previous cases taken from manuscript sources, see Van Caenegem, *Writs*, pp. 72–4.

45 Van Caenegem, *Writs*, pp. 69–71.
46 *Anglo-Saxon Writs*, pp. 252–6, 480–2; cf. C. R. Hart, *The Early Charters of Eastern England*, Studies in Early English History, ed. H. P. R. Finberg, V (Leicester, 1966), nr 44, p. 38, with the date 'c. 1055'.
47 *English Justice*, pp. 14–15; in the same sense: Turner, 'Origins of the medieval English Jury', pp. 9–10.
48 G. D. G. Hall, *Eng. Hist. Rev.* 76 (1961), 316–17.
49 Harmer, *Anglo-Saxon Writs*, p. 481.
50 J. Bosworth and T. N. Toller, *An Anglo-Saxon Dictionary* (London, 1898), p. 94; *Supplement* (Oxford, 1921), p. 86; J. R. C. Hall, *A concise Anglo-Saxon Dictionary*, 4th edn with suppl. by H. D. Meritt (Cambridge, 1960), p. 45. See also the *Oxford English Dictionary*, I (1933), 829.
51 'And þese lewedemen hit sworen after þanne þat it was bitold þe two del in to Sancte Benedicte in to Rameseie and þe Þriddendel Sancte Botulfe in to Þorneie … þurulf Þe fissere of Farshevede and Lefstan Herlepic of Witleseye, heo sworen þe þriddendel in to þorneie, and Lefsi Crevleta and Ailmer Hogg' of Wellen and Wulfgeit þe fissere of Heytumdegrave he sworen al to del in to Rameseye (*Cartul. Ram.*, I, 188 and III, 38–9, and Red Book of Thorney Abb., II, fol. 372, see n. 53).
52 The original meaning of *disrationare* is given as 'speaking, discussing, expounding one's reasons, pleading', by R. Besnier, 'Vadiatio legis et leges, *Rev. hist. droit français et étranger*, 4th ser., 19/20 (1940–1), 103.
53 See Van Caenegem, *Writs*, pp. 69–71. The texts are in W. H. Hart and P. A. Lyons, *Cartularium monasterii de Rameseia*, Rolls Series, I (London, 1884), nr cxv, p. 188 and nr dxliv, *ibid.*, pp. 38–9; Macray, *Chronicon abbatiae Rameseiensis*, pp. 166–7; Red Book of Thorney, II, fol. 372 (Cambridge Univ. Library, Add. Ms. 3021).
54 *Origins of medieval English Jury*, p. 10.
55 N. D. Hurnard, 'The jury of Presentment and the Assize of Clarendon', *Eng. Hist. Rev.* 56 (1941), 374–410.
56 Glanvill, II, 7, ed. G. D. G. Hall, p. 28.
57 Yver, 'Le "Très Ancien Coutumier" ', p. 356, prudently writes that the substitution of a recognition for a duel at the request of the defendant has 'many chances of being based on a ducal legislative act': although the *Très Ancien Coutumier* does not in this case use the expression *statutum est*, the fact that this procedure was known in Normandy as the *bref d'establie* suggests that it was based on a ducal *stabilimentum* or *établissement*, i.e. an ordinance. Besnier, ' "Inquisitiones" et "Recognitiones" ', pp. 200–1, is inclined to believe in usage rather than legislation as the source of this institution in Normandy. So popular was the jury in Normandy that even Church courts used it, see the cases of 1142–63 and 1153 quoted in Haskins, *Norman Institutions*, pp. 223–5.
58 *Norman Institutions*, pp. 198–216; in the same sense: Besnier, 'Le procès pétitoire', pp. 384–6.
59 Haskins, *Norman Institutions*, pp. 216–17.
60 See the remarks of Boussard, *Le Gouvernement d'Henri II Plantagenêt*, p. 293. The case in the king's court at Gavray in 1159, where Osmond son of Richard Vasce 'on oath of lawful men proved his right to presentation' is equally unconvincing as proof of a general use of recognitions 'as a matter of right', in spite of Haskins' different impression (*op. cit.*, p. 218).
61 See the survey by Yver, 'Le "Très Ancien Coutumier" de Normandie',

NOTES TO PAGES 84-7

NOTES TO PAGES 84-7

pp. 333–74. The author gives an exhaustive list of eleven 'actes législatifs du règne de Henri II, mentionnés par les chroniques et actes de l'époque', but some of these acts are administrative measures concerning the levy of taxes and others deal with one single topic or their contents are vaguely described by such phrases as 'injuriam nemini facere' and 'pacem tenere'.

62 Edited by Léchaudé-d'Anisy, see n. 34.

CHAPTER 4 PAGES 85–110

1 Thus Richardson and Sayles, *Governance*, p. 388.

2 R. David, *Les grands systèmes de droit contemporains*, 3rd edn (Paris, 1969) (Eng. edn: R. David and J. E. C. Brierley, *Major Legal Systems in the World Today*, London, 1968).

3 See the excellent studies on 'England's First Entry into Europe' and 'The Place of England in the Twelfth-Century Renaissance' in R. W. Southern, *Medieval Humanism and other Studies* (Oxford, 1970), pp. 135–57, 158–81, and also the same author's article on 'The Place of England in the Twelfth-Century Renaissance', *History*, 45 (1960), 201–16. The see of Canterbury was one of the main gates through which continental influence entered England. On this see R. Foreville, 'Naissance d'une conscience politique dans l'Angleterre du 12e siècle', *Entretiens sur la Renaissance du 12e siècle*, ed. by M. de Gandillac and E. Jeauneau (Paris/The Hague, 1968), pp. 179–208. The continentals who had taken over the English Church also took over its ancient quarrels. As Professor G. W. S. Barrow put it: 'What could be more normal – and yet what, when one thinks of it, more odd – than the spectacle of the continental Thurstan from Condé-sur-Seulles fighting vigorously in defence of the ancient church of York against the continental Raoul d'Escures fighting for Canterbury, the continental John fighting for Glasgow, the continental Bernard fighting for St. David's, while overshadowing them and moderating their adopted squabbles lay the heavy hand of the continental Henry of Normandy, determined to lose no jot or title of the rights of the Anglo-Saxon crown?' (*Eng. Hist. Rev.* 81 (1966), 372).

4 Published posthumously in 1837 by E. Gans.

5 E. H. Gombrich, *In search of Cultural History*, The P. M. Deneke Lecture 1967 (Oxford, 1969), pp. 9–10.

6 See on the *Volksgeist*, which as *l'esprit de la nation* appeared among one of fourteen factors in Montesquieu and was turned into the one source of all law by Savigny, and on the historical school of jurisprudence: H. Kantorowicz, 'Volksgeist und historische Rechtsschule', *Histor. Zeitschrift*, 108 (1912), 295–325 (= *Rechtshistorische Schriften*, ed. by H. Coing and G. Immel, Freiburger Rechts– und Staatswissenschaftliche Abhandlungen, 30, pp. 435–56) and H. Kantorowicz, 'Savigny and the Historical School of Law', *Law Quarterly Review*, 53 (1937), 326–43 (= *ibid.*, pp. 419–34), also P. Caroni, 'Savigny und die Kodifikation', *Zeitschrift der Savigny-Stiftung für Rechtsgeschichte*, 86, G.A. (1969), 133–50. The enthusiasm for the *Volksgeist* was shared by Hegel and Savigny and many others in Germany in the early nineteenth century.

7 Thus the (supposed) absence of a taste for risks and love of adventure in the southern Netherlands was invoked to explain the separation of

the northern and southern Netherlands in the late sixteenth century. See E. Lousse, 'Some chapters in the constitutional history of Belgium', *Schweizerische Beiträge zur allgemeinen Geschichte*, 14 (1956), 52.

8 F. W. Maitland, *English Law and the Renaissance*, Rede Lecture (Cambridge, 1901), p. 23.

9 C. K. Allen, *Law in the Making* (3rd edn, Oxford, 1939), p. 88.

10 F. Wieacker, *Privatrechtsgeschichte der Neuzeit* (2nd edn, Göttingen, 1967), p. 498 writes that the legal system has marked the national character more strongly in Anglo-Saxon countries than anywhere else.

11 R. Pound, *Interpretations of legal history*, Cambridge Studies in English Legal History (Cambridge, 1923). The 'economic interpretation' is one of a choice of six, the others being the ethical and religious, the political, the ethnological and biological, the 'great-lawyer' and the engineering interpretations. The book is based on a series of lectures given in Cambridge in 1922.

12 See an excellent comparison of the two systems of civil procedure in M. Cappelletti, *Processo e ideologie* (Bologna, 1969), pp. 287–338, ch. ix: 'Il processo civile italiano nel quadro della contrapposizione "civil law"–"common law". Appunti storico-comparativi'.

13 See the remarks of Pound, *Interpretations*, pp. 56–9.

14 See the useful survey of J. Vanderlinden, *Le concept de code en Europe occidentale du XIIe au XIXe siècle. Essai de définition* (Brussels, 1967).

15 The first part of the *Très Ancien Coutumier de Normandie* is of c. 1204, the second part (where the terms of the Norman writs are given for the first time) of c. 1220. The *Grand Coutumier de Normandie* or *Summa de Legibus* is of the middle of the century. Outside Normandy the oldest French law-book is Pierre de Fontaines's *Conseil à un ami* of the same time as the *Summa*. Pierre de Fontaines worked *inter alia* in the Norman Exchequer in Rouen; his work is strongly marked by Roman law, while the Norman *coutumiers* were hardly influenced by it, see J. Brejon de Lavergnée, 'La pénétration du droit romain dans les pays de l'Ouest de la France', *Recueil de Mémoires et Travaux publiés par la Soc. hist. droit et instit. des anciens pays de droit écrit*, 6 (1967), 55–61.

16 On the institutions of the Norman kingdom of Sicily see the remarkable book of M. Caravale, *Il Regno Normanno di Sicilia* (Milan, 1966).

17 See the discussion of this point in Van Caenegem, *Writs*, pp. 380–6, the Introduction in Hall's edition of Glanvill, particularly pp. xxxvi–xxxviii, and Richardson and Sayles, *Law and Legislation*, pp. 71–87. Glanvill was so clear and methodical because he focused his attention on one great office of state, like Richard fitz Neal had done ten years before, when he described the working of the Exchequer. Miss Adams, reviewing Lady Stenton's *English Justice* in *Speculum*, 41 (1966), 374, looks for 'influence of Roman principles like that of prompt reseisin and not pleading while disseised', but anyone who cares to study Ruffini's *Actio spolii* knows that these two rules are early medieval and have nothing to do with the Bolognese revival of the *Corpus Juris*.

18 That Bracton's knowledge of the civil law was profound has recently been elucidated, after a long controversy, by Professor S. E. Thorne in the Introduction to *Bracton. On the Laws and Customs of England*, ed. by G. E. Woodbine, trans. by S. E. Thorne, I (Cambridge, Mass., 1968), pp. xxiv–xlviii, and more briefly in S. E. Thorne, *Henry de Bracton 1268–1968* (Exeter, 1970), a commemorative lecture.

19 There is at present no general history of European law, but the reader will find a vast amount of information in the *Continental Legal History Series*, I: *A General Survey* (London, 1912) and VII: *A history of continental civil procedure*, by A. Engelmann and others (London, 1928), where contributions by many leading legal historians are brought together in translation. An excellent broad survey will be found in F. Calasso, *Medio Evo del Diritto*, I: *Le Fonti* (Milan, 1954) and in Wieacker, *Privatrechtsgeschichte der Neuzeit*. The latter although concentrating on Germany is European in outlook and begins with the origins of European jurisprudence in the Middle Ages.

20 The success of Placentinus in England was pointed out by P. Legendre, 'Miscellanea Britannica', *Traditio*, 15 (1959), 491, n. 2.

21 P. Legendre, 'Un nouveau manuscrit du Pseudo Ulpien de Edendo', *Tijdschr. v. Rechtsgeschiedenis. Rev. d'Hist. du Droit*, 24 (1956), 61, going back to older ideas, seems to prefer 1113–20 or even the beginning of the century. A.-M. Stickler in *Dictionnaire de Droit Canonique*, VI (Paris, 1957), col. 1135 is doubtful and prefers some date after Gratian (1140). M. Conrat, *Geschichte der Quellen und Literatur des römischen Rechts im früheren Mittelalter*, I (Leipzig, 1891), 615 and M. Caillemer, *Le droit civil dans les provinces anglo-normandes au XIIe siècle*, Mémoires de l'Acad. de Caen (Caen, 1883), pp. 170–4 place the work after Gratian and towards the middle of his century.

22 See van Caenegem, *Writs*, pp. 360–90. In the following years we mention the *Tractaturi de judiciis* of c. 1170, the *In principio de ordine judiciario* of c. 1171, the *Rhetorica Ecclesiastica* of shortly before 1179, the *Olim edebatur*, possibly by Otto of Pavia, of after 1177, Johannes Bassianus's *Quicumque vult* of 1167–81, the *Ordo Bambergensis* of 1182–5, the *Practica* of William Longchamp of 1183–9, the *ordo Cum essem Mutinae* of Pillius of c. 1184–98 and the *Summa de ordine judiciorum* of Ricardus Anglicus of 1196. Some of the dates differ from the traditional ones and are taken from the recent study by K. W. Nör, 'Päpstliche Dekretalen in den ordines iudiciorum der frühen Legistik', *Ius Commune*, 3 (1970), 1–9. Also see Stickler in *Dictionnaire de Droit Canonique*, VI, cols. 1135–7. The great classical works are all well known, Tancred's *Ordo* of 1214–16, Roffredus Beneventanus's two *libelli* of 1227–35 and 1237–1243, William of Drogheda's *Summa* of 1239 and William Durand's *Speculum* of 1272 (1st version) and 1287 (2nd version).

23 C. Duggan, *Twelfth-century Decretal Collections and their importance in English history*, University of London Historical Studies, XII (London, 1963), 26; La Due, *Papal Rescripts*, pp. 44, 46; Southern, *Western Society and the Church*, p. 117. On Ralph Niger's criticism of Roman law see p. 101, n. 67.

24 The history of the bishops' courts in England still has to be written, but I feel supported by the words of Miss Sayers that 'allusions to procedural troubles in the Church courts, both ordinary and delegated, of the 1150s occur in John of Salisbury's letters, which show that the outline of the ordo judiciarius was not yet developed, uniform, or fully understood' (*Papal Judges Delegate*, p. 46). Kantorowicz reminds us that the procedural treatises of the twelfth century were far ahead of practice (H. Kantorowicz and W. W. Buckland, *Studies in the glossators of the Roman Law* (Cambridge, 1939), p. 72).

25 C. R. Cheney, *English Bishops' Chanceries 1100–1250* (Manchester, 1950), p. 20. Cheney, *From Becket to Langton*, p. 147: 'in the third

quarter of the twelfth century the *officiales* of bishops are mentioned in general terms, then in the last two decades named individuals appear with the title'. Cf. the conclusion in E. Rathbone, 'Roman Law in the Anglo-Norman Realm', *Studia Gratiana*, 11 (*Collectanea S. Kuttner*, I) (Bologna, 1967), 263: 'There is therefore evidence of some degree of familiarity with the principles and doctrines of Roman law in a fairly wide stratum of the educated class in England about 1180 and of a marked infiltration in court and council by men with specialist knowledge.' Much research remains to be done on the spread of the new procedure in the actual *practice* of the European Church courts, but I would be surprised if it took place on any important scale before the beginning of the thirteenth century; theoretical knowledge does not necessarily lead to application in court practice. See the remarks to that effect in Scammell, *Hugh du Puiset*, pp. 70–1 and N. Adams in *Speculum*, 41 (1966), 374.

26 Duggan, *Decretal Collections*, p. 69. The Anglo-Norman school of canonists belongs to the late twelfth and early thirteenth centuries, see S. Kuttner and E. Rathbone, 'Anglo-Norman canonists of the twelfth century', *Traditio*, 7 (1949–51), 279–358; Le Bras, Lefebvre and Rambaud, *L'âge classique*, pp. 287–90; Duggan, *Decretal Collections*, pp. 110–17; Rathbone, 'Roman Law in the Anglo-Norman Realm', pp. 255–271.

27 W. Kienast, 'Die Anfänge des europäischen Staatensystems im späteren Mittelalter', *Histor. Zeitschrift*, 153 (1936), 153; the author says 'the intensification of state activity which started in Normandy, Flanders, England and Sicily, and then in the French crown domain, led, if I may say so, to a feudal absolutism; from this significant development the German kingdom as such drew no permanent profit, only the rising territorial principalities profited from this new phenomenon'. The reader will find J. R. Strayer, *On the Medieval Origins of the Modern State* (Princeton, 1970) very rewarding. See on the rôle of the time factor and the importance of England's early political unification in this context: Plucknett, 'Roman Law and English Common Law', pp. 48–50.

28 J. R. Strayer and R. Coulborn, 'The Idea of Feudalism', *Feudalism in History*, ed. R. Coulborn (Princeton, 1956), p. 9. England was well placed to leave the feudal for the bureaucratic stage, as soon as the monetary resources and the professional people which the Carolingians had so cruelly lacked were available in the twelfth century.

29 See Lyon and Verhulst, *Medieval Finance*.

30 F. Wieacker, 'Fritz Pringsheim zum Gedächtnis', *Zeitschr. der Savigny-Stiftung für Rechtsgeschichte*, 85, R.A. (1968), 601–12.

31 *Cambridge Law Journal*, 5 (1935), 347–65 (repr. in Pringsheim's *Gesammelte Abhandlungen*, I (Heidelberg, 1961), 76–90). See the remarks and bibliography in Cappelletti, *Processo*, pp. 288ff.

32 On this point we now have the monograph of Peter, *Actio und Writ*.

33 Pollock and Maitland, *History of English Law*, II, 558.

34 The address *Francis et Anglicis* is current until the end of the century and occurs frequently in documents that deal with purely English affairs, so it clearly relates to the Normans and the English in England and not to the inhabitants of Normandy and those of England. I am afraid that the different view in Southern, *Medieval Humanism*, p. 142, is not confirmed by the documents.

35 Stenton, *English Society*, p. 269.

36 The Dialogue was begun in 1176/7 and probably completed in its original form before Easter 1179.
37 Johnson, *Course of the Exchequer*, p. 53: 'Nowadays, when English and Normans live close together and marry and give in marriage to each other, the nations are so mixed that it can scarcely be decided – I speak of freemen – who is of English birth and who of Norman, except, of course, the villeins.'
38 Historians played an interesting part in reviving English national feeling by rehabilitating the Anglo-Saxon period. See Southern, 'The Place of England', pp. 208–18 and K. Schnith, 'Von Symeon von Durham zu Wilhelm von Newburgh. Wege der englischen "Volksgeschichte" im 12. Jahrhundert', *Speculum Historiale*, ed. C. Bauer, C. Boehm and M. Müller (Munich, 1965), pp. 242–56; this author finds that in William of Newburgh, writing at the end of the twelfth century, the opposition is no more between English and Normans but between the *'Angli'* and the Welsh and Scots; he also finds that William of Newburgh shows that English and Normans had at last been united. The influence of those historians made itself felt in the legal field, see W. Ullmann, 'On the influence of Geoffrey of Monmouth in English History', *op. cit.*, pp. 257–76.
39 This feudal character remained strong throughout the centuries. See the warning in Blackstone's *Commentaries on the Laws of England*, II (new edn, London, 1813), 46: 'It is impossible to understand with any degree of accuracy, either the civil constitution of this kingdom, or the laws which regulate its landed property, without some general acquaintance with the nature and doctrine of feuds or the feudal law.'
40 Le Patourel, 'The Plantagenet Dominions', p. 295, has some striking phrases about this.
41 Pipe Roll 15 Henry II, p. 149. Some people are amerced 'quia petierunt assisam sicut liberi et fuerunt rustici'. Poole, *Obligations of Society*, p. 13, writes: 'The sharp distinction between freemen and villeins begins to emerge in the twelfth century with the growth of royal writs and possessory assizes ... The lawyers are striving in the face of great difficulties to reduce the whole population into the simple classification, free or serf, *aut liberi aut servi*. Ultimately they were successful in degrading most of the peasants into a condition of serfdom.' It is striking that Charlemagne had also tried to enforce this simple and basic classification in his *Responsa misso cuidam data* of 802–13: 'non est amplius nisi liber et servus' (A. Boretius and V. Krause, *Capitularia Regum Francorum*, M.G.H., LL., I (Hanover, 1883) nr 58, p. 145, c. 1). There are two aspects in Henry's policy. It is true that the unfree population was excluded – but was it practically possible to give the whole population direct access to the royal courts and was it politically feasible to do this over the heads of the landowners? On the other hand Henry II gave equal protection to all free men, notably the humble against the powerful, as is stressed in Glanvill and in the Norman *coutumiers*. There was a long tradition in the Middle Ages of alliance between the crown and ordinary freemen against the aristocracy.
42 Winfield, *Chief sources*, pp. 8–13. From the start French was the language spoken in the central courts. In the local courts English could have won but they were dwarfed by the royal courts and at the end of the thirteenth century the fate of English as a legal language was sealed. Even in local courts, where the parties might talk in English, their

pleaders used French and so from the late thirteenth century onwards did many law-writers. A Statute – in French – of 1362 tried in vain to revive English. Equally vain was Cromwell's attempt in 1650 to impose English as the language of the law. It was finally realized by a Parliament of George II in 1731.

43 S. A. Riesenfeld, 'Individual and family rights in land during the formative period of the common law', *Essays in Jurisprudence in Honor of Roscoe Pound*, ed. R. A. Newman (New York, 1962), p. 450, rightly believes that 'until the loss of Normandy in 1204 and for some time thereafter the Conquest resulted broadly speaking in parallel developments on both sides of the Channel and the growth of feudal institutions showed no fundamental variations in both parts of the monarchy'.

44 Southern, *Medieval Humanism*, p. 140.

45 Most of the bishops in the period 1170–1213, who often came from the royal household, the Exchequer or the judicial bench, 'seem to have belonged to Anglo-Norman families... they present a more English look at the end of the period than at the beginning' (Cheney, *From Becket to Langton*, p. 27). Also in the middle of the twelfth century the clergy in England 'had perhaps been less disposed to think about their Englishry than at other periods, for they were often educated in France or Italy, many of them were of French origin, they looked for ecclesiastical preferment both at home and abroad'. It was the loss of Normandy that sharpened the separation from France and 'encouraged national sentiment to grow in the English Church' (*ibid.*, p. 101).

46 Southern, *Medieval Humanism*, p. 155.

47 The nine-hundredth anniversary of the battle of Hastings has led to several assessments of its cultural results. D. J. A. Matthew, *The Norman Conquest* (London, 1966), for example, concludes: 'The Normans succeeded in suppressing a culture that was superior to their own but what finally triumphed was not the Norman element, but a compromise between the various contenders in the arena' (pp. 290, 296).

48 The Petition of the Barons at the Parliament of Oxford in 1258, c. 6, shows their determination that English heiresses shall not be married where they are 'disparaged' i.e. to men who do not belong to the English nation (Stubbs, *Select Charters*, p. 374: Item petunt de maritagiis domino regi pertinentibus quod non maritentur ubi disparagentur, videlicet hominibus qui non sunt de natione regni Angliae).

49 Pound, *Spirit of the Common Law*, p. 39; Maitland, *English Law and the Renaissance*, pp. 52–4. Wyclif thought it preferable to 'lerne and teche þe kyngis statutis and namely þe Grete Chartre þan þe emperours lawe or myche part of þe popis'.

50 F. Pollock, *The Expansion of the Common Law* (London, 1904). Pollock also praised a quality in the English 'national character' 'which has never been fully acounted for: we prefer to call it practical wisdom' (p. 58).

51 The study of 'national sense' or feeling is difficult. For an interesting attempt to date the beginning of French national feeling, placed in the early fourteenth century, see B. Guenée, 'Etat et nation en France au moyen âge', *Revue Historique*, 237 (1967), 17–30: the feeling was that 'un état solide doit s'appuyer sur une nation' (p. 19) and the beginning of the fourteenth century was 'the decisive moment, when the members of the political community which the kingdom is, became convinced that they formed at the same time an ethnic community, a nation'

(p. 21). See also some initial remarks about the 'nation' and the 'English people' in Cam, *Law-Finders*, p. 195.

52 A. Duck, *De usu et authoritate iuris civilis Romanorum in dominiis Principum Christianorum* (Leiden, 1654), fol. *2: Ius Civile Romanorum coelitus datum esse communiter et jure meritoque creditur (publishers' dedication).

53 *Potter's Outlines of English Legal History*, 5th edn by A. K. R. Kiralfy (London, 1958), Introduction, p. 1.

54 Walter Map, *De Nugis*, ed. Th. Wright (London, 1850), p. 227: 'inusitati judicii subtilis inventor'.

55 Pound, *Interpretations of legal history*, p. 101.

56 Painter, *English feudal barony*, p. 193.

57 See, for example, on the paltry legislative efforts of this reign Y. Bongert, 'Vers la formation d'un pouvoir législatif royal (fin XIe–début XIII siècle)', *Etudes offertes à J. Macqueron* (Aix-en-Provence, 1971), pp. 127–40; things did not improve until the early thirteenth century, under Philip Augustus.

58 See *inter alia* Kuttner and Rathbone, 'Anglo-Norman canonists'; Poole, *From Domesday Book to Magna Carta*, pp. 232–64; Southern, 'The Place of England'; Richardson and Sayles, *Law and Legislation*, pp. 71–87; Rathbone, 'Roman Law in the Anglo-Norman Realm'; Southern, *Medieval Humanism*.

59 Rathbone, 'Roman Law in the Anglo-Norman Realm', p. 259.

60 W. Ullmann in *Revue Belge de Philologie et d'Histoire*, 48 (1970), 77, draws attention to the sudden end of this 'brisk traffic of English students to Bologna and its University at the turn of the twelfth and thirteenth centuries, a traffic which, as far as one knows, almost abruptly ceases in the first half of the thirteenth century'.

61 Richardson and Sayles, *Governance*, p. 271.

62 See van Caenegem, *Writs*, pp. 365–70; from time to time new traces are discovered of the early penetration of modern law-books into England, see P. Legendre, 'Miscellanea Britannica', pp. 491–7; id., 'Recherches sur les commentaires pré-accursiens', *Tijdschr. v. Rechtsgeschiedenis*, 33 (1965), 353–429; id., 'Droit romain médiéval', *Rev. hist. droit français et étranger*, 4th ser., 42 (1964), 136–8; G. Fransen and P. Legendre, 'Nouveaux fragments de la "Summa Institutionum" de Placentin', *ibid.*, 44 (1966), 115; N. R. Ker, *Pastedowns in Oxford Bindings*, Oxford Bibl. Soc., N.S. 5 (Oxford, 1954), nrs 46, 133, 249 etc. See also Rathbone, 'Roman Law in the Anglo-Norman Realm', p. 257. How quick this penetration was can be realized if one compares it with a similar analysis for Belgium where the new learning turned up a good deal later in the catalogues, see R. C. van Caenegem, 'Ouvrages de droit romain dans les catalogues des anciens Pays-Bas méridionaux (XIII–XVIe siècle)', *Tijdschr. v. Rechtsgeschiedenis*, 28 (1960), 297–347, 403–38, and R. C. van Caenegem, 'Notes on canon law books in medieval Belgian book-lists', *Studia Gratiana*, XII (*Collectanea S. Kuttner*, II) (Bologna, 1967), 267–92.

63 At the end of Henry II's reign in the case prepared for the monks of Christ Church in their action against Archbishop Baldwin there were 93 citations of the *Decretum*, 44 of the Digest, 39 of the Code, 5 of the Institutes and one of the *Authenticum*, according to Richardson and Sayles, *Governance*, p. 319.

64 Duggan, *Decretal Collections*, pp. 120ff., the proportion of English

decretals diminishes after 1185, because the mainly English primitive collections were used less, cf. C. R. Cheney, 'England and the Roman Curia', p. 186. The 1170s were 'the one phase in which English initiative exercised a crucial influence on the development of canon law for the universal Church' (p. 146).

65 See the excellent ch. xv: *'Statecraft and Learning'*, in Richardson and Sayles, *Governance*, pp. 265–84, who stress (p. 269) that 'the secularisation of learning – or perhaps literacy would be the better word – made possible Henry's achievement and gave it permanence'. Certain towns, which founded their own schools, were rebuked and these schools forbidden as 'adulterine', because they clashed with ecclesiastical interests (Stenton, *English Society*, pp. 258–9).

66 See Richardson and Sayles, *Governance*, pp. 214–15; Stenton, *English Justice*, pp. 82–7; Richardson and Sayles, *Law and Legislation*, pp. 71–87.

67 Rathbone, 'Roman Law in the Anglo-Norman Realm', pp. 256–7; Niger expressly names the *pauperistae*; cf. H. Kantorowicz, 'An English Theologian's view of Roman Law: Pepo, Irnerius, Ralph Niger', *Medieval and Renaissance Studies*, 1 (1941), 237–51 (repr. *Rechtshistor. Schriften*, pp. 231–44), with an edition of the passage in question, dated 1179–89. Niger studied at Paris and was a Master of Arts by 1168 at the latest. He was a pupil of Gerard la Pucelle, the theologian and canonist, and was a royal courtier. There is no evidence that he himself did formal law studies.

68 S. Kuttner, 'Dat Galienus Opes et Sanctio Justiniana', *Linguistic and Literary Studies H.A. Hatzfeld*, ed. by A. S. Crisafulli (Washington, 1964), p. 237.

69 The famous expression appears in Luther's *Tischreden* (Weimar ed., III, 2809*b*, also VII, 7030 and V, 5663, where it is called 'an old saying that is true', but it surely is an old popular expression, see A. Stein, 'Martin Luthers Meinungen über die Juristen', *Zeitschr. der Savigny-Stiftung für Rechtsgeschichte*, 85, K.A. (1968), 362–75.

70 Ullmann, 'On the influence of Geoffrey of Monmouth', pp. 257ff. The papal letter begins with the statement that the king had asked for Roman law texts.

71 See the very interesting discussion between A. Marongiu, 'A model state in the Middle Ages: the Norman and Swabian Kingdom of Sicily', *Comparative Studies in Society and History*, 6 (1964), 307–20 and J. R. Strayer, 'Comment', *ibid.*, pp. 321–4. The adage 'conditor et interpres . . .' is from Vacarius (p. 312).

72 See the praise of Henry II's strength and justice in Walter Map, *De Nugis Curialium*, ed. M. R. James (Oxford, 1914), p. 277.

73 P. H. Sawyer, 'The Wealth of England in the Eleventh Century', *Trans. Roy. Hist. Soc.*, 5th ser., 15 (1965), 145–64.

74 Painter, *English feudal barony*, p. 170.

75 See some interesting figures in Painter, *ibid.*, pp. 121–38.

76 Richardson and Sayles, *Law and Legislation*, p. 97.

77 G. O. Sayles, *The Medieval Foundations of England*, University Paperbacks (London, 1966), p. 304, cf. in the same sense p. 326; in Richardson and Sayles, *Governance*, p. 181, we are, however, invited not to refuse 'to allow the king a higher motive also, for he is, in a very real sense, the fountain of justice'. Cronne, *Stephen*, p. 247 notes that Henry I was known as the 'Lion of Justice' but reminds us 'that the lion is a beast of prey' and writes that 'it can be seen with the utmost clarity

in almost every membrane of the one surviving pipe roll of Henry's reign that justice was exploited as a source of profit'.

78 J. A. Giles, *Petri Blesensis Opera*, I (Oxford, 1846), nr 66, p. 192.

79 See, for example, *Ludwig van Beethoven. Briefe. Eine Auswahl*, ed. H. Schaefer (Berlin, 1969), nrs 27 (A.D. 1804), 44 (1809), 122 (1822) and 141 (1824): it is strange to see Beethoven writing to his publisher that for 'his mass [opus 86] alone he could get as much as 100 florins' (nr 44, to Breitkopf & Härtel), the Missa Solemnis he put at 1,000 fl. and the Ninth Symphony at 600 florins (nr 141).

80 See the reflections on the cost of administration and justice in Southern, *Western Society and the Church*, p. 113: 'It would be wrong to think that governments sought jurisdiction mainly for the income it provided, for most of the income was swallowed up by the officials who worked the judicial machinery. The real reason why governments sought jurisdiction was because it was the only practical way in which they would enforce their claims to lordship. But once the process had started, the officials who were created by the process had a strong interest in keeping it going'; cf. the remarks on the 'needlessly cynical' profit-theory in Matthew, *The Norman Conquest*, p. 272.

81 Poole, *Obligations of Society*, p. 79: there were 574 named criminals; under the Assize of Northampton 705 were condemned and their chattels yielded a total of £343, the average per person amounted to 10s. 11d. and 9s. 8d. respectively. Poole concludes that 'we shall not be far wrong if we assume that the goods and chattels, the net personalty, of the ordinary peasant was about 10s.'

82 J. H. Ramsay, *A history of the revenues of the kings of England 1066–1399*, I (Oxford, 1925), 191; D. C. Douglas, *English Historical Documents*, II: *1042–1189* (London, 1953), 56; Painter, *English feudal barony*, p. 170. Douglas mentions the increase in the profits of royal justice under Henry II, but also points out that 'the expenses of government were rapidly increasing'.

83 Those of 1176 were particularly fierce and within a year had yielded £4,613 14s. 11d. (Ramsay, *Revenues*, I, 124). The following year they yielded about £5,500 – see Pipe Roll 23 Henry II. They do not include the amercements paid by the clergy, which for some reason do not appear in the rolls (H. Mayr-Harting, 'Henry II and the Papacy 1170–1189', *Journ. Eccles. Hist.* 16 (1965), 48) nor, of course, those paid *in cameram*.

84 This was, for example, the revenue from the archiepiscopal see of York (kept vacant by Henry II for eight years) paid into the Exchequer, see H. Mayr-Harting, *op. cit.*, p. 49. Hubert Walter, as archbishop of Canterbury could count on a net income of £1,100 to £1,800 a year from the temporal possessions of the see, see C. R. Cheney, *Hubert Walter* (London, 1967), p. 50.

85 See the case of the testament of a London woman, Leofgifu, involving King Edward the Confessor and his queen, in Barlow, *Edward the Confessor*, pp. 177–8. The author remarks: 'This was justice of a sort, and exactly the sort which was expected in the eleventh century. Every interested party took his cut. There is no doubt that on most occasions gifts were offered to the king or queen and accepted.' Hugh the Chantor in his *History of the Church of York* (ed. Johnson, p. 29) explains that the bishop of Durham tried to influence Henry I in favour of the elect, Thomas of York, by promising 1,000 marks of silver. He did not

forget the queen, who was offered ten per cent of this sum. And the earl of Chester's mother, Countess Lucy, in 1130 accounted for £266 13s. 4d. for the land of her father and 500 marks for the privilege of remaining unmarried for five years and a further 45 marks for making the agreement. She also accounted for 20 marks to the queen 'who customarily had her percentage on private bargains made with the king' (Cronne, *Stephen*, pp. 231–2). To speak of 'corruption' would probably be an anachronism, for, as Richardson and Sayles, *Governance*, p. 374, put it 'it was not yet thought reprehensible to smooth the course of the law'.

86 *Dialogus de Scaccario*, ed. C. Johnson (London, 1950), p. 2.

87 To say that the Common Law was a freak event in western history is stating a historical fact – history has its freaks just as nature. It detracts in no way from the admiration one feels for this deviation from the common European pattern and the global importance it acquired in modern times.

88 Few authors have stressed the time factor in this context, but see the remarks of M. Smith, *A General View of European Legal History and other Papers* (New York, 1927), pp. 28–9. Also, Cam, *Law-Finders*, p. 163, points out its importance in the history of representative institutions and the peculiar place of the English parliament and she concludes 'it is the timing in England that differs from that of the Continent'. Cf. my own arguments in 'L'histoire du droit et la chronologie. Réflexions sur la formation du "Common Law" et la procédure romano-canonique', *Etudes G. Le Bras*, II (Paris, 1965), 1459–65.

89 See the remarks of Dawson, *Lay Judges*, pp. 44–7 on the hesitations in thirteenth-century France as to what choice to make, notably between the *enquête* of Frankish origin and the Romano-canonical modes of proof. In many countries there has been a transitional period between the archaic law of the early Middle Ages and the adoption of Roman law and Romano-canonical procedure. During this period experiments with native elements were made, but only in England did these experiments lead to a permanent system.

90 The time factor explains why Roman law was excluded. It does not explain why the void was filled by a system based on royal justices, writs, the forms of action, and recognitions, but this I tried to elucidate in the previous chapters.

91 R. Besnier, *La Coutume de Normandie. Histoire externe* (Paris, 1935), p. 16. On the law of Normandy as the least romanized of all French *coutumes*, see Plucknett, 'Roman Law and English Common Law', p. 28: Plucknett finds Frankish but no Roman law in twelfth-century Normandy and notes that 'the *Très Ancien Coutumier* is as little given to Romanesque erudition as our own Glanvill'. On the early Common Law as essentially feudal law, see W. Ullmann's remarks in *Principles of Government and Politics in the Middle Ages* (2nd edn, London, 1966), pp. 166–8.

92 *England in the reign of King Henry the Eighth. A Dialogue between Cardinal Pole and Thomas Lupset, by Thomas Starkey*, ed. J. M. Cowper, Early English Texts Society, Extra Series, XII, II (London, 1871), 194. The Dialogue is from c. 1538. An edition in modernized English was published in 1948 by K. M. Burton. On this passage see Holdsworth, *History*, IV, 259 and Maitland, *English Law and the Renaissance*, pp. 41–6.

93 The law on default is a striking example of the survival of archaic attitudes in the Common Law till this day. For centuries the Common Law remained loyal to the idea of the old Germanic process that litigation without the presence of plaintiff and defendant was impossible (as impossible as having a football match without one of the teams). No judgment could be given unless the defendant appeared. The law could put pressure on him, seise his goods, threaten outlawry, but not give judgment for the plaintiff; this became possible in the eighteenth century, and then always against the defaulter.

94 The works on 'historical laws' are innumerable. A good selection is listed in Dahlmann-Waitz, *Quellenkunde der deutschen Geschichte* (10th edn, Stuttgart, 1969), 4/118–34.

95 See the remarks of R. W. Southern, 'Aspects of the European tradition of historical writing, I: the classical tradition from Einhard to Geoffrey of Monmouth', *Trans. Roy. Hist. Soc.* 5th ser., 20 (1970), 175, 181.

96 J. Needham, *The Grand Titration. Science and Society in East and West* (London, 1969), p. 216. We find a similar sentiment in J. Dhondt, 'Henri Pirenne: historien des institutions urbaines', *Annali della Fondazione Italiana per la Storia Amministrativa*, 3 (1966), 128: 'Mais enfin, penser au hasard en histoire, c'est au mains s'éloigner de la notion de recurrence et même abandonner la notion d'une histoire accessible au raisonnement. C'est donc le point que Pirenne avait atteint en 1933' (when Pirenne lectured on chance in history). It is noteworthy that Dr Needham, in his *Clerks and Craftsmen in China and the West* (Cambridge, 1970), p. 17, takes a more positive attitude towards the rôle of 'a series of historical accidents' by which 'perhaps (though their geographical and social determinism remains to be worked out)' modern science developed.

97 I. Berlin, *Four Essays on Liberty* (Oxford, 1969), p. 1.

98 Dhondt, 'Henri Pirenne', pp. 126–9.

99 J. Monod, *Le hasard et la nécessité. Essai sur la philosophie naturelle de la biologie moderne* (Paris, 1970); see especially p. 127: 'Nous disons que ces altérations sont accidentelles, qu'elles ont lieu au hasard. Et puisqu'elles constituent la seule source possible de modifications du texte génétique … il s'ensuit nécessairement que le hasard seul est à la source de toute nouveauté, de toute création dans la biosphère. Le hasard pur, le seul hasard, liberté absolue mais aveugle, à la racine même du prodigieux édifice de l'évolution, cette notion centrale de la biologie moderne n'est plus aujourd'hui une hypothèse parmi d'autres possibles ou au moins concevables. Elle est la seule concevable, comme seule compatible avec les faits d'observation et d'expérience.' The reader will also find some thoughts on chance in history in N. Chiaromonte, *The Paradox of History* (London, s.d.), based on a series of lectures given in 1966.

100 See the remarks on events in various European countries in Dawson, *Lay Judges*, p. 302, who writes: 'None of these developments was inevitable. None needed to occur, certainly on so great a scale.'

101 The exceptional position of the crown and the crisis of the local courts, which we saw in the first chapter, led to the elimination of the local justices and the amazing supremacy of the central courts. But for those circumstances new rules and concepts might have been introduced in the existing courts, and a very different legal situation might have been produced. In the county of Flanders, for example, the second half

of the twelfth century also witnessed a striking modernization of procedure, but it all came about in the existing courts, notably in the courts of the powerful towns, and in no way led to the expansion of the *curia comitis*. In England the will to modernize law and procedure coincided with a crisis in the local administration of justice.

102 See the remarks in Ullmann, *Principles of Government*, pp. 151ff.

103 See the important pages on 'the constitutional significance of the feudal relationship and its bearing on the individual in society' in Ullmann, *Individual and Society*, pp. 51–98.

104 Pound, *Spirit of the Common Law*, p. 63: 'In the seventeenth century it was progressive to insist upon the royal prerogative. Those who thought of the king as the guardian of social interests and wished to give him arbitrary power, that he might use it benevolently in the general interest, were enraged to see the sovereign tied down by antiquated legal bonds discovered by lawyers in such musty and dusty parchments as Magna Carta.'

105 See Ch. Ogilvie, *The King's Government and the Common Law 1471–1641* (Oxford, 1958).

106 Opinion in England at the time was divided: while some believed the Common Law to be the ancient free constitution from Anglo-Saxon times, others decried it as the bad law, brought by the tyrannical Normans, see Hill, *Puritanism and Revolution* (2nd edn, London, 1965), pp. 58–125; D. Veall, *The popular movement for law reform 1640–1660* (Oxford, 1970).

107 Although a medievalist can hardly help remembering Isidore of Seville's phrase about Britain as 'Oceani insula interfuso mari toto orbe divisa' (*Etymologiae*, XIV, VI, 2).

108 I borrow this simile from the excellent description of the transformation undergone in Scotland by the justiciar of Anglo-Norman origin, see G. W. S. Barrow, 'The Scottish Justiciar in the twelfth and thirteenth centuries', *The Juridical Review* (1971), p. 133.

Index of
Persons, Places and Subjects*

* Anglo-Saxon, England (English) and Normandy (Norman) have been omitted.

149

Fortescue, Sir John, 98
Franca elemosina, 48
France, French, 5–14, 18, 23, 24, 32,
34, 37, 59, 70, 71, 82*d*, 85–90,
95–8, 101*h*, 105, 108–10, 139
n27, 141 n45, 145 nn89, 91
language, 5, 85, 95, 95*c*, 97, 105,
140, n42
Franchise, 10
Franci, 4, 93, 95, 139 n34
Frankalmoin, 16, 42, 48, 126 n79,
127 n81
Franks, Frankish, 7–11, 15, 32, 41,
65, 73–5, 78, 79, 90, 93, 107,
116 n69, 145 nn89, 91
Frederick II, German king, Roman
emperor, 90
Freeman, E., 6, 7, 111 n12
Fulk le Réchin, count of Anjou, 86*a*
Fyrd, 5

Gaul, 109
Gavray, 135 n60
Geoffrey, William son of, 128 n94
George II, 140 n42
Gerard la Pucelle, 143 n67
Germanic, 44, 65, 88, 89, 96*d*, 102,
105, 108, 131 n7
Germany, German, 7, 10, 11, 32,
86, 88, 101, 108, 138 n19, 139
n27
Gewere, 44
Gewrit and insegel, 116 n72
Gilbert, Walter Fitz, 38, 40
Glanvill, 1, 18, 20, 22, 25, 44, 46, 48,
50, 54, 57, 59, 92
on Assize of Windsor, 81–3
and European authors, 90
first Common Law treatise, 30, 33
and the Institutes, 18
on *nemo tenetur*, 27
and Roman law, 91, 102
on unwritten laws, 2–3
Glanvill, Ranulf de, 21, 61
Glasgow, bishop John, 136 n3
Gloucester, abbey, 37, 128 n96
abbot, 128 n98
Miles of, 20
Walter of, 121 n48
Godstow, abbey, 76
Gollinton, Peter of, 128 n94
Gombrich, E. H., 86
Gotse, Richard son of, 115 n55

Grand Coutumier de Normandie, 137
n15
Gratian, 3*a*, 120 n40, 138 n21, 142
n63
Greece, Greek, 87, 93
Gregory VII, 3*a*
Grim, Edward, 116 n69
Guenée, B., 141 n51

Hailes, Simon of, 38
Hall, G. D. G., 54, 77, 78
Hallmoot, 76, 96
Harmer, F. E., 31, 77, 78, 112 n18,
118 n11
Harrold priory, 38, 119 n31
Haskins, C. H., 57, 83, 134 n37
Hastings, 7, 141 n47
Heatherslaw, 51, 127 n93
Hegel, 86, 87, 95, 107, 136 n6
Heiresses, marriage of, 141 n48
Henry I, king, 18, 19, 26, 37, 39*c*, 51,
52, 55, 76, 95*c*, 111 n1, 114 n48,
115 n55, 128 n97, 129 n110, 136
n3, 144 n85
and justices in eyre, 13, 15, 20, 22,
82
and local justices, 14, 15, 25,
113 n31
Henry II, king, 2, 3, 14, 26, 33, 35,
36, 39, 48, 52, 61, 73, 75, 76,
84, 91, 96, 97*e*, 100, 101, 104,
108, 115 n53, 118 n17, 122 n56,
124 n68, 125 n71, 126 nn75, 80,
127 n93, 133 n29, 140 n41, 142
n63, 143 nn65, 72, 144 n82
and advowson, 49, 49*h*
and central courts, 15, 23
and Inquest of Sheriffs, 18, 43*e*
and the jury, 79, 80
and justices in eyre, 19, 20, 82
and the Justiciar, 113 n29
his legislation, 42, 43, 46, 69, 70,
72, 83, 122 n52, 135 n61
and seisin, 40, 41, 44, 45
and villeinage, 55
wealth of, 102, 103
Henry VIII, king, 2, 106
Henry II, German king, 8
Herbert, Alexander son of, 77
Hereford Cathedral, 76
Herefordshire, 20
Heresy, 132 n18
Herlepic, Lefstan, 135 n51